LIVING
WORDS

LIVING
WORDS

From the
Writings of
FRANK C. LAUBACH

Compiled by F. Elmo Robinson

ZONDERVAN PUBLISHING HOUSE
GRAND RAPIDS, MICHIGAN

WORDS TO THE READER

There is spiritual dynamite in the thoughts contained in this little book. These thoughts have been gleaned from the writings of Dr. Frank C. Laubach. They have fired his soul and made him a world-renowned Christian leader and teacher with profound spiritual insights, and have made him the apostle of literacy to millions of illiterates the world over.

Through these many years, hosts of people have read, been inspired and challenged by the writings of Dr. Laubach. But the urgent need right now is that the tremendous thoughts which have fired the soul of this great man should fire the souls of millions of men and women everywhere.

With this need in mind, these basic thoughts, elaborated in the writings of Dr. Laubach, have here been brought together under 70 headings. But the potential might of these revolutionary truths must be released. To accomplish this readers will need to saturate their minds and hearts with these great truths through deep and prolonged meditation on them.

FOREWORD

In 1930, at the beginning of my literacy career, I was writing letters to my father from a lonely spot in Lanao, Philippines. My father printed them in a local weekly newspaper, and Constance Padwick, a missionary editor in Cairo, selected the best for a booklet. They are called *Letters of a Modern Mystic.* It seems they have affected more lives than all my speeches.

Now in 1965, at the last end of my life, Mr. F. Elmo Robinson has poured love and prayer and fine discrimination into the selection of all I have written. The result is this book which you have in your hands. It will be interesting to see whether Elmo Robinson has done again what Constance Padwick did thirty-five years ago, and whether the public will respond now as it did then. Elmo has at least succeeded in one thing—he has brought tears to my eyes as I am reminded of the aching, and sometimes tormented and broken heart, from which these burning words were torn.

And now what is the conclusion of the whole matter? At eighty what matters?

Before me on the wall are three pictures of Jesus. One, woven into a Persian rug, shows Jesus holding a rescued lamb. Another pictures Jesus stretching out His hands and saying, "Come unto me." The third shows Jesus pointing toward the whole world and saying, "Feed my sheep."

What matters at eighty? No question seems important save this:

Jesus Christ, did You rise? This is the most important question in this universe for us humans. Are You *here?* Are You at work finishing Your kingdom? Everything—our philosophy, our deeds, our treatment of one another, our reason for living— hinges upon whether You are *here* continuing the kingdom purpose which You began in the first century. If You are here, unseen, at work, our job is to keep in perfect atunement with You, and help You. Your interpretation of the meaning of the universe is the best we can conceive. It has achieved the greatest benefit. It has the best hope of success. No other meaning gives hope.

So we implore You to make us surer, surer every day, so that we can make other people surer every day. Atheists want us to believe that we are worshiping a projection of ourselves and of the West. Prove to me and my fellows that this is false, that You are really *here.*

Then show us how we may help You with Your kingdom of love. We do not want to get off the track. We want to be clear channels.

How can we help You take this planet and make it the kind of planet it ought to be? Is this belief in a better world true? Is the "Great Society," the Christian ideal? Is the elimination of poverty the Christian goal? Or, desirable as these things are, do people need most your forgiveness, and peace, and love? Only so, will your purpose be fulfilled? Will this help You fulfill Your purpose?

In John Masefield's drama *The Trial of Jesus,* Procula, the wife of Pilate hears the report that Jesus rose from the tomb. She asks Longinus, a Roman soldier, in great excitement: "Do you think He is dead?"

Longinus replies: "No, I don't."

Procula asks: "Then where is He?"

And Longinus replies: "Loose in the world, lady, where neither Jew nor Roman nor anyone else can stop Him!'

He will mold every event, every power, from Wall Street to communism, for His kingdom purpose. For He is "loose in the world, lady, and nothing can stop Him!"

This then, is the conclusion of the whole matter: "Be not afraid, follow Me, feed My sheep. I have overcome the world."

FRANK C. LAUBACH

KEY TO CITATIONS

A. *Learning the Vocabulary of God*
B. *Channels of Spiritual Power*
C. *Christ Liveth in Me*
D. *Letters by a Modern Mystic*
E. *Prayer, the Mightiest Force in the World*
F. *You Are My Friends*
G. *The World Is Learning Compassion*
H. *A Call to Spiritual Advance*
I. *Wake Up or Blow Up*
J. *How to Teach One and Win One for Christ*
Note: Some of the citations included in this little book have been taken from the earlier editions of the books and pamphlets of Dr. Frank C. Laubach.

CONTENTS

CONTENTS

LIVING
WORDS

CHRISTIANITY IS AN
EXPERIMENTAL RELIGION

Beloved, believe not every spirit,
but try the spirits whether they are
of God (I John 4:1a).

We are trying an experiment: We are, in this book, calling on God and listening for an answer and letting experience tell us whether it works. It is as justifiable an experiment as any experiment in science. And it is like all psychological experiments; it must be worked out in the laboratory of our own minds and souls.

Nearly everything in the Christian religion is experimental. We rightly call it an "experimental religion." It starts with authorities whose wonderful loves and deep integrity makes us admire and trust them; we see in them more radiant and wonderful lives than other people have, and we want to be like them. We ask them why they are this way, and they tell us they got it from Jesus Christ and the Father. We want to live that way, so we try getting in touch with God to see whether it works with us.

Before a scientist tries an experiment, he must have faith in the work of those who already have reported success.

That is all the faith we need in order to begin our experiment with "divine imagination." We know that imagination precedes everything that any man ever creates . . . So, for a better world, we need more people holding better thoughts.

Again, we know that when we listen, our highest imagination seems to be something better than we are. It seems like something from God. You do not know this when you begin, but you come to understand it as your experiment progresses. I did; I know you will. A greater number of people every day are finding that this kind of experimental religion takes them far beyond where scientists who are out of contact with God have ever gone (B. pp. 92, 93).

EXPLORERS IN THE REALM OF THE SPIRIT

> I gave my heart to seek and search out by wisdom concerning all things that are done under heaven: this sore travail hath God given to the sons of man to be exercised therewith (Ecclesiastes 1:13).

Explorers in the realm of the spirit are like Columbus when he landed on a new continent and did not know what lay beyond. We probably have only just reached the outskirts of prayer. A vast unknown continent lies beyond us to be explored, conquered and cultivated. Nothing is so thrilling as discovery. Every Christian can and should join in the highest of all adventures in the most wonderful of all worlds, the world of the spirit. Nobody need leave home nor give up his work, for he has his mind with him every minute, and it is in the mind that this exploration is carried on.

The electrical wizard Steinmetz said the greatest discoveries of the twentieth century would be in the realm of the spirit. He is right—and *only* those who pray will make these discoveries. Heaven knows that we need these discoveries now, for we are in the midst of a war to control men's minds. Some of us are tingling with the zest of adventure, for over every hill and around every corner new breath-taking surprises greet our eyes. Adventuring in prayer is exciting fun. God is *there* ahead of us when we walk out in His direction, and God loves surprises and endless variety (E. pp. 50, 51).

God, thank Thee for the freshness of discovery, which lends zest to every day, when I listen to Thy voice and wait until Thou leadest . . . Thine, all Thine, nothing but Thine, walking through the doors Thou dost open, obeying instantly! (A. p. 20).

God, experience proves that a minute *with* Thee *always* brings fruit, often wonderful fruit; experience proves that a minute apart from Thee is wasted or full of thoughts of malice or vice. *Abide* in Me as the branch *abides* in the vine. *It abides all the time*, every moment . . . Hard, but essential. Think Thy thoughts, God here all day—Thine, *not* mine (A. p. 31).

THIS DAY, THIS HOUR CAN BE WONDERFUL

This is the day which the Lord hath made; we will rejoice and be glad in it (Psalm 118:24).

The most wonderful discovery that has ever come to me is that I do not have to wait until some future time for the glorious hour. I need not sing, "O that will be glory for me—" and wait for any grave. *This hour* can be heaven. *Any* hour for *any* one can be as rich as God!

I asked, "God, how wonderful dost Thou wish this hour alone with Thee to be?"

"It can be as wonderful as any hour that any human being has ever lived... I am not only willing to make this hour marvelous. I am in travail to set you akindle with the Christ-thing which has no name. How fully can you surrender and not be afraid?"

And I answered:

"Fill my mind with Thy mind to the last crevice. Catch me up in Thine arms and make this hour as terribly glorious as any human being ever lived, if Thou wilt.

"And God, I scarce see how one could live if his heart held more than mine had had from Thee these past two hours."

Will they last? Ah, that is the question I must not ask. I shall just live this hour on until it is full, then step into the next hour. Neither tomorrow matters, nor yesterday. Every *now* is an eternity if it is full of God (D. pp. 15, 16).

Any hour of any day may be made perfect by merely choosing. It is perfect if one looks toward God that entire hour, waiting for His leadership all through the hour and trying hard to do every tiny thing exactly as God wishes it done, as perfectly as possible. No emotions are necessary. Just the doing of God's will perfectly makes the hour a perfect one. And the result of that one perfect hour, I believe, will echo down through eternity (D. p. 19).

CHRIST IN
THE CENTER TODAY

I am crucified with Christ: nevertheless I live; yet not I, but Christ
liveth in me: and the life which I now
live in the flesh I live by the faith of
the Son of God, who loved me, and
gave himself for me (Galatians 2:20)

God, if You rule every movement, You will be inside my eyes
directing them. The eyes are the windows of the soul. If You are
in my eyes, men will see You there and call You *Love*. Then my
life will be love with a picture of Christ in the center; Christ
bearing a cross and wearing thorns, and with anguish in His
heart. *That* love will bless everyone and harm no one (A. p. 6).

Compassion for the multitudes burned strongly in Christ. You
seldom find it on the pages of history, except where it was
started through Jesus Christ. The other great religions contain
the Golden Rule, but that rule lacks the power to drive men to
compassionate service . . .

All religions accept Jesus as a man who once lived and gave
us the Golden Rule. But a dead Jesus is not enough. The power
of Jesus lies *in His presence here now as risen Lord* . . .

We can, and we must, work with people who do not believe
this, but our hope must lie in those who have a far more
profound experience of Him as the living Christ. Compassion
will flow from the hearts of those who have Christ in their own
lives . . .

The only hope of this evil, selfish world is for the living Christ
to abide in enough of us to change the spiritual climate of the

19

world. He alone is able to change greed to compassion, fear to faith, and hate to love (B. pp. 22, 23).

But that is only half of the story. When He enters into us *we become a part of the way*. God's highway runs straight through us! We become *His* physical bodies. That was the meaning of Paul when he wrote in Ephesians 3:19, 20 "I pray that you may be filled full of God." When His power works in us He is able to do far more than we dare to ask or even think (B. pp. 22, 23, 24).

GIVING GOD A CHANCE

> If my people, which are called by my name, shall humble themselves, and pray, and seek my face, and turn from their wicked ways; then will I hear from heaven, and will forgive their sin, and will heal their land (II Chronicles 7:14).

God is always awaiting the chance to give us high days. We are seldom in deep earnest about giving Him His chance...

Oh, if we *only* let God have His *full* chance He will break our hearts with the glory of His revelation (D. pp. 33, 41).

I do not for an instant doubt that if we let God have His own way, all of us would... discover that our hands and tongues and eyes are big, "big because of the plan," because God who dwells in them has a secret plan of the things He will do for the world, using their hands and bodies and eyes and minds.

The Risen Lord is working. We open our doors; He enters and rolls up His sleeves and goes on with His work—through us! This is what Paul meant when he said: "God working through us is able to do unutterably more..." Unutterably more than we ever could do alone, and more than He could do without us. We need God, and *God needs us* (C. p. 21).

"*All things are possible with God.*" They are possible *with* God, but not for us alone. When we try for a little while a day to become channels of God we are unable to see much result. The reason is obvious, so obvious that perhaps we miss it . . .

Examine that sentence again: "All things are possible *with* God." It doesn't say, "All things are possible *for* God." It means that God exerts more power when you work with Him. Jesus may have implied, "*when* you help God." The Scripture does not make it clear whether the word "with" means "if you and God *work together.*" Evidently God, by Himself, is not doing all things that need to be done in the world (B. pp. 164, 165).

WALKING WITH GOD THIS DAY

Thou wilt shew me the path of life: in thy presence is fulness of joy; at thy right hand there are pleasures for evermore (Psalm 16:11).

Into my heart, into my heart;
Come into my heart, Lord Jesus;
Come in today, come in to stay,
Come into my heart, Lord Jesus.

I shall try to keep You in my mind every moment of my waking hours. I shall try to let my hand write what You direct. I shall try to let You be the speaker and direct my every word. I shall try to let You direct my acts. I shall try to learn Your language as it was taught by You and all others through whom You speak—in beauty and singing birds and cool breezes, in radiant Christlike faces, in sacrifices and tears. It will cost not only much, but *everything that conflicts with* this resolve . . .

O Christ, Your lovely words, Your lovely deeds are not beyond my understanding. And when I think of You, Your love begins to burn in my heart. I must be like You, seeking need and trying to help every minute. I have tried in vain to know why need exists. But this I know and it is enough: that I must seek need, and love and help . . .

Need is Your language, is a word from You. How to approach this problem is baffling. Unsolved problems are Your language, for in them You are our schoolmaster training us to be Your children (A. pp 5, 6, 7).

All of us need to develop the spiritual ear that will enable us to hear God's voice. We also need to learn His language so that we will know what He is saying when we hear Him. He doesn't speak the English language all the time. He doesn't even use words all the time when He speaks to us . . . He uses sights, sounds, smells, tastes, thoughts, beauty, sorrow, friends, indeed, every incident in life to speak to those who are able to understand His language (B. p. 142).

CHRIST COMES IN IF . . .

If a man loves me, he will keep my words and my Father will love him, and we will come unto him, and make our abode with him (John 14:23).

Why is not Christ in all our hearts all the time? He does not come into our hearts unless we invite Him in. He says: "Behold, I stand at the door and knock; if anyone hears my voice and opens the door, I will come in . . ." But there is one condition on which He *will* come in. Paul said: "Do you not understand that Christ lives in you *if* . . . ?" There is an "if." Some people who read these pages will say, "I have no experience of Christ inside me." They are right. He is not inside because they have not obeyed the "if". . . .

What is that "if"? I John 4:12 tells us very plainly. "If we love one another, God abides in us." "God is love, and he who abides in love abides in God, and God abides in him"(4:16). "He who does not love does not know God; for God is love" (4:8). I John 3:17 says, "If any one has the world's goods and sees his brother in need, yet closes his heart against him, how does God's love abide in him?" So love is one "if."

But there is another "if." I John 3:24 says: "All who keep his commandments abide in him, and he in them." Keeping these commandments is the other "if" (C. pp. 10, 11).

When Christ's Spirit enters and mingles with our spirit, the reborn soul has a *reborn will*. It is not a *new birth* unless it is a *new will*. This new will loves to do the will of God, just as Christ loves to do God's will. Christ's nature transforms ours. We no longer want to sin. The old son of Adam could not obey; the new son of God loves to obey. I John 3:9 says:"Anyone who is born again is a child of God and does not commit sin. God's nature is in him. He cannot live in sin because he is born again and is God's child."

From the moment He enters, we dwell together for the rest of our lives in this same house . . . It is His house and it is mine—it is ours! "And so we dwell together, my Lord and I" (C. pp. 18, 19).

GOD IS
SPEAKING

I have not spoken in secret, in a
dark place of the earth . . . I the
LORD speak righteousness, I declare
things that are right (Isaiah 45:19).

The most important discovery a human being ever makes is
that God can speak to him. When one makes this discovery it
reorganizes his entire life. If he can hear God he can tap the
source of all truth and all wisdom. God did speak to the
characters in the Bible; that is the reason that we look on the
Bible as an authority (B. p. 142).

Not only is God speaking to us every moment and everywhere, but He is also doing everything He can to help us. In
Romans 8:28 Paul says, "We know that in everything God
works for good for those who love him." And I think Paul might
have ended his sentence more quickly, "In everything God
works with good," not only in those who love Him but ultimately
in those who do not. If they are not following His will He works
to bring them back to follow His will, and if that involves suffering on their part so that they will turn away from wrong, that will
prove to be a benediction to them also (B. p. 154).

There is a warning needed, however, at this point. We must
forever be on our guard against cocksureness that what we
heard was really the voice of God. We have a subtle and
dangerous tendency to mix His pure message with wishful
thinking. We instinctively hope that God will talk to us about
ourselves . . . You have often read that God is forever seeking to
carry us *past ourselves*. We, on the other hand, are forever
seeking to drag God down to ourselves . . . We are going to find

the larger life by losing the little life—the little life which seeks self. God calls us to pour ourselves into world need (B. p. 158).

Hearing God speak is, as we have said in a previous chapter, not a matter for a few minutes but a matter for all day every day. We shall grow better and better and better at it. We must look for God and listen for God in every transaction and pleasure and problem of the whole day (B. p. 148).

LEARNING
TO LISTEN

I will hear what God the LORD will speak: for he will speak peace unto his people, and to his saints: but let them not turn again to folly (Psalm 85:8).

We have been talking about how God speaks. We need to ask ourselves, "How do we hear?" How do we use that key that opens the floodgates heavenward? We do it in prayer, and it is much simpler than we usually think. It does not require some erudite supermind like that of Gerald Heard to tell us how to do it. A little old woman in a rocking chair, if she knows her Lord, can understand it just as well as some spiritual or intellectual giant. We need not strain, we need not use exactly the right words, we need not put our bodies in the right posture. Indeed, paying much attention to form deadens our ear to God. All we need is faith. We *believe*, then we simply say to the Unseen whom we expect to be near us and to answer us, "Lord, what have You to say to me?" And He answers. At first His answer may not be very clear. That is because we are not yet familiar with God's voice and do not know whether it is God speaking. When God spoke to the boy Samuel he thought it was Eli speaking! The great mistake we make is to give up too soon. It is the experience of the saints that they often have to wait an hour or two before they are sure that they hear God. "Take time to be holy," applies when we are trying to hear God. Remember, He is in you. Or, if you prefer, the Holy Spirit is in you, and you and He are listening to the Father (B. pp. 160, 161).

All day I see souls dead to God look sadly out of hungry eyes. I want them to know my discovery! That any minute can be paradise! That any place can be heaven! That any man can have God! That every man does have God the moment he speaks to God, or listens for Him! (D. p. 24).

Wait, listening for Him to speak. Do not crowd God; do not wait in eager impatience, but in patience, to hear Him and to do what He tells you to do. It is impossible to record what comes to you, just as it would be to record all the thoughts that crowd into the mind in a day. God talks just as fast and just as naturally as we think (B. p. 157).

THROUGH TRIALS
TO TRIUMPH

Now thanks be unto God, which always causeth us to triumph in Christ, and maketh manifest the savour of his knowledge by us in every place (II Corinthians 2:14).

We are ourselves on trial with Jesus. He could walk into the jaws of death to do His blessed work for others. He could dare to speak out against wrong and take the consequences. He could receive floggings, could allow men to spit in His face, could endure the agony of thorns in His head, could be taunted without a word or even a thought of anger, could think of His mother while writhing on the cross, could cry, "Father, forgive them, for they know not what they do" . . . Tragedy, magnificent horror! The best Man who ever lived dying because He was too good to run away . . .

The God who would allow the drama to stop there would be either a monster or dead. "My God, why? . . ."

So we cannot believe in a good God unless we have Easter. It is a difficult story to believe, because we have had nothing else quite like it before or since. But it is only the difficulty of believing the unprecedented. On the other hand to doubt it is far more difficult. I must either rule out the whole story of the life of Jesus or else rule out any intelligence or heart from the universe (D. pp. 41, 42).

Jesus does not answer why we have evil and why we suffer . . . But He did for us what was most important: He showed us how to rise above evil, and trouble, and to transform them into character. He showed us how to squeeze triumph out of them, to wring hope out of despair, bliss out of pain, friendship out of loneliness, and victory out of death (F. pp. 100, 101).

Thanks be to God, which giveth us the victory through our Lord Jesus Christ (I Corinthians 15:57).

YIELD, AND KEEP YIELDING TO GOD

Commit thy way unto the LORD; trust also in him; and he shall bring it to pass (Psalm 37:5).

In his great picture, *Christ Knocking at the Door,* Holman Hunt has painted the door without a latch on the outside. That is like the door of our hearts; the responsibility to open the door rests with the inner man . . .

God is inviting us to be His sons, and God's first step in making us sons is to entrust us with an immensely important decision. The soul has such amazing freedom that it can say "yes" or "no," *even to God who made it!* What an astounding conception! (F. p. 33).

The maker of worlds put wee, two-legged creatures on this tiny planet of a second-rate sun, put souls in those wee creatures, set these souls free, and then began gently to knock at the doors of their hearts begging them to open and let Him come in and do them greater good! Every second He sustains their lives, sees to the very center—yet will not enter the inner soul until we open the door. He came and clothed Himself in flesh to woo our affection. He let men torture and crucify His body; He suffered and suffers when men refuse to let Him enlarge and glorify them.

This amazing story is just a little beyond our comprehension, and yet we grasp enough of it at times—at those moments when our souls hunger and thirst—enough of it to fling ourselves weeping into Thine arms, as I do now, O incomprehensible, incredible Love! (A. p. 67).

"Here I am, take me. Take all of me...I mean to do what Thou commandest, I mean to spend all my hours obeying Thy will. I will follow, as the disciples followed, without knowing where Thou wilt lead. I repent, because my past has been so full of wrecked resolves, so wicked, and weak, and disappointing. But Thou hast called me. Thou art eager to change me. Now I give Thee all I know how to give. I am not strong, but I lean on Thy promise to give me strength" (F. p. 54).

CHRIST'S LOVE
ENLARGES US

That Christ may dwell in your
hearts by faith; that ye, being rooted
and grounded in love, May be able
to comprehend with all saints what
is the breadth, and length, and depth,
and height; And to know the love of
Christ, which passeth knowledge, that
ye might be filled with all the fulness
of God (Ephesians 3:17, 18, 19).

. . . Lovers are eager to get away by themselves and to be left
alone. To them, engrossment in one another becomes the
supreme virtue, and other people are largely forgotten.

To be in love with Jesus has exactly the opposite effect, if one
understands Jesus. For scarce does His love suffuse us, but we
feel it reaching out from us in an effort to help others to know
our Friend. As we come under His spell He stretches our small
minds wider and ever wider until at last we shall have a love as
wide as the wide world—as wide as His own (F. p. 72).

We have a thermometer by which we may judge our likeness
to Jesus. This thermometer is the heat of our compassion and
the wideness of our love. When we become perfectly Christlike
we shall search every face for an opportunity to help and help
and help all day long (F. p. 75).

No individual is an absolute terminal of the love of Jesus. He
reaches through us toward others. Indeed He is not satisfied
with us until He has made us as eager to reach out and help
others as He Himself is to reach them. When a piece of iron
touches a magnet the iron itself becomes a magnet. This is what

happens to us when we touch Jesus—we begin to draw men toward Him.

The simple program of Christ for winning the whole world is to make each person He touches magnetic enough with love to draw others. This "each-one-catch-one" endless chain, this geometrical progression of love would, He believed, continue to draw all men into his happy circle (F. p. 80).

LEARNING THE
COMPASSION OF JESUS

> And Jesus went forth, and saw a great multitude, and was moved with compassion toward them, and he healed their sick (Matthew 14:14).

The noblest statement of the Old Testament about man's duty to man was uttered by Micah: "... what doth the Lord require of thee, but to do justly, and to love mercy; and to walk humbly with thy God?" That was the highest ethical level reached before Jesus.

But when Jesus came, He demanded far more!

Every day of His life, He himself went much further than doing justly and loving mercy and walking humbly. Every day He was out on the road hunting for people who needed help, and helping them wherever He found them. That was the way He lived, and that is the way He demands that His followers live ...

The noblest characters before Jesus had taught a benign good will toward men, no matter how weak or wicked they might be. But the compassion of Jesus was not just a benign good will toward weakness and evil. He loved men too much to leave them as they were, or to wink at their weakness and sins. He had a passionate yearning for men to be born again, for they were not good enough. He loved people for what He could make out of them, for their possibilities, for the perfect pattern which they had failed to attain. He loved them so much that He wanted them to fulfill their destiny—to become magnificent sons of God (G. pp. 24, 25).

Many Christians are suffering from slow death of the soul because they are not helping God reach others ... This practice of lifting people to God has got to be intense and energetic and constant. If we have one hundred friends who are hostile to it, that means that our zeal must be one hundred times as great for our way of life as theirs (B. pp. 174, 175).

"YE MUST BE BORN AGAIN"

Therefore, if any one is in Christ, he is a new creation; the old has passed away, behold, the new has come (II Corinthians 5:17).

"Ye must be born again" was a new idea clothed in the oldest of words. Our souls, Jesus saw, are not yet "alive" until this "new birth" occurs ...

The new birth means far more than being "intellectually convinced." Even if we say, "Lord, Lord, I accept thee as my Saviour," that is not enough. We must make an unconditional surrender all the way down the line. Inside yourself there must take place a transformation in every corner of your intricate and many-sided nature. It is a stupendous achievement for Christ to capture even one soul thus completely (F. pp. 51, 52).

When Jesus of Nazareth began to make the world over into the kingdom of God, He started something so vast that the one human body of Jesus was not enough. His one body could walk only in Palestine. At Pentecost the Spirit of Christ entered 120 persons, and then Christ had 120 bodies. But 120 were not enough. Outside Damascus, Christ entered Saul of Tarsus. Then He entered hundreds, then thousands. Even that many were not enough for the vast world task before Him. He is *not* finished until His love captures *every* heart and fills every body. The whole race must become His body, and the sons of man together become the dwelling place of the Son of man . . .

If Christ is continuing to do the work which He began to do when He walked as Jesus of Nazareth in Palestine, we may expect any surprise. We never know what wonderful thing may happen next.

So! When He comes in and starts business, we are likely to be surprised by any kind of miracle! Diseases may vanish with our prayers. Mountains may be moved. The world may applaud. One has every reason to stand on tiptoe with expectancy. For God loves surprises, and He can do anything. William Carey's motto is right which says "Expect great things from God. Attempt great things for God" (C. pp. 27, 29).

TRUE PRAYER
CHANNELS GOD'S POWER

If ye abide in me, and my words abide in you, ye shall ask what ye will, and it shall be done unto you (John 15:7).

Prayer must begin with self, but prayer must not end with self, it must pass on through the self to others . . . prayers . . . are miserable if they end in self (H. p. 13).

Prayer for others is the first, simplest, mightiest channel in the world (B. p. 104).

Right praying, Jesus repeatedly declared, can remove mountains, can accomplish anything (E. p. 11).

Whenever a thing is right but impossible, that is the time to pray! Jesus Christ never toned down His prayers, His thoughts or His deeds to other people's standards of the "possible." He did the impossible easily because He did what God desired. We don't have to compromise with the second bests—our poor second bests!—not if we know how to pray! What is troubling you? Leave it to God. It isn't impossible for Him (B. p. 121).

Pray for everyone who needs prayer. If anyone merits condemnation, he needs prayer. If anyone has sinned and suffered, he needs prayer. If anyone has treated me badly, he needs my prayer, not my resentment. If anyone is carrying a heavy load of responsibility, he needs my prayer. If I disapprove of his methods or ideas or his politics, he needs my prayer. Briefly, pray for others, for all others that come to mind.

Do that, and power will slowly accumulate, power to bless and sweeten and heal the world. How much power? No one knows. But the Source of that power created the universe! And "with God nothing is impossible." We are in quest of the impossible . . .

Not delightful feelings, not health, must be our high aim, but to bring the world to Christ—then *power* flows in and through and out like "rivers of living water!" (H. pp. 14, 16).

CHRIST CAN
HEAL YOU NOW

Call unto me, and I will answer
thee, and shew thee great and mighty
things, which thou knowest not (Jere-
miah 33:3). For I am the LORD that
healeth thee (Exodus 15:26b).

Those caught in the coils of intolerable disease and pain
beyond the reach of medical science desire relief and cure; they
are not satisfied by explanations. What, if anything, can Jesus do
for them? They want a straight answer. So this is the answer:
He desires to cure our bodies, and He will do it if we yield Him
full faith and full surrender. This He promised over and over
again. He never refused to cure any person who came to Him.
He never doubted that it was the Father's will for them to be
well. He was *sure,* and He cured at once! (F. p. 24).

Until we can bring ourselves to total absorption in Christ we
do not know what potential powers of healing may lie unsus-
pected within us, dormant because we do not half measure up
to our possibilities (F. p. 135).

The sick person must be (1) perfectly receptive and (2)
perfectly responsive. Remember what Jesus said: "Thy faith hath
made thee whole." The patient must be perfectly willing for
God to heal him so that his will and God's will merge into
one; then the arc closes and the healing flows like a current of
electricity (F. p. 125).

It is plain at least that during the time when Peter, Stephen,
Philip, and Paul were healing, they were in a rapture of
ceaseless obedience to the Spirit . . .

"But what shall I do, here and now," asks some sick man, "to be relieved from this agony?"

This is what you must do: be sure, from the very bottom of your subconscious mind, that Christ heals today. That is the fundamental requisite, as far as you are concerned (F. p. 135).

Of course you are not good enough, but then no one is good enough . . . He accepts your yielding instead of goodness. Without yielding, *no one* is good enough. By yielding, *everyone* is good enough . . .

Now you know, yet you need to read this over until you know with your subconscious mind (F. p. 137).

WORKING
WITH GOD

We are labourers together with God (I Corinthians 3:9).

Everyone realizes that at times we are definitely helping God, but few realize how much God depends on us to help Him. Many people help God without ever thinking about Him. The Bible says that God used Cyrus, the ancient Babylonian king, although Cyrus knew nothing of God . . .

We are helping God, and He is helping us, and the two of us together are helping the world. Thus it becomes literally working *with* God . . .

Helping God means that we understand Him, what He is doing, what He likes, what He dislikes, what He is. And that means that we must walk and talk and live with Jesus daily because, as Jesus said, "He who has seen Me has seen the Father."

No man ever really sees the Father except in the life of Jesus. This is exactly what Jesus said Himself, and it is true. We have seen gods, but we have not seen the Father of Love except in the face of Jesus Christ.

So we help God by understanding Jesus Christ, and then we help Him by praying and listening.

The third way in which we help God is by helping others, asking nothing in return. The man who is helping others for a price may get the price, but he spoils the gratitude and love which would come if he had not driven his bargain . . .

Most people will help if a need is called to their attention. They let God come to them and do the asking. But the New Testament does not teach that. It says: "Go ye into all the world and preach the gospel to every creature . . ."

Isaiah 6 records a wonderful vision in which Isaiah saw the Lord "high and lifted up on a throne." And he heard a voice saying, "Whom shall I send? Who will go for us?" And Isaiah answered, "Here am I, send me."

That is what God is looking for—people who will pray until God speaks and then will say, "Here am I, send me" (B. pp. 163, 168, 170, 171, 175).

LEARNING THE
VOCABULARY OF GOD

> The heavens declare the glory of
> God; and firmament sheweth his handy-
> work. Day unto day uttereth speech,
> and night unto night sheweth knowl-
> edge (Psalm 19:1, 2).

No one else speaks so constantly or says such wonderful things
to us as Jesus, once we have learned His vocabulary. If we do
not hear Him speaking to us today, it is not because He is silent,
but because we are ignorant of His language . . .

Anything which calls us from wrongdoing, which fires us with
His purpose, enkindles love, or whispers peace into the troubled
heart, is the voice of Christ—anything with a message for the
soul (F. pp. 42, 44).

This search for the vocabulary of God gives new meaning to
many Bible verses. Open before me are the words of Luke 8:18
and 21: "Take heed therefore how ye hear" and "My mother
and my brethren are these which hear the word of God, and do
it." To hear and do *perfectly* would be like Jesus. It would mean
purity in the deep recesses of thought.

God, help me to welcome each day as a game with circumstances, to conquer the obstacles which rise like fog to shut You
out. They call out new strength of will and so develop that
strength. Teach me, God, to try hardest when I want to try
least. Make me hottest in soul when the environment is coldest,
for their sakes who are cold (A. pp. 10, 11).

If, as we believe, Christ *is* the *way*, the *truth* and the *life*,

37

then one way for us to see with clear eye is to saturate ourselves day after day in Christ and His teaching, to walk with Him across the pages of the four gospels until we instantly and instinctively look at every question from His viewpoint. Then His word that bears on every question will leap to our lips (A. p. 88).

JESUS MADE LOVE PURE

Seeing ye have purified your souls in obeying the truth through the Spirit unto unfeigned love of the brethren, see that ye love one another with a pure heart fervently (I Peter 1:22).

Jesus revealed a pure spiritual love, warmer and more appealing than all the passion of earthly lovers. He has made purity beautiful. He has made love so pure and spiritual, has given it such a divine definition, that His beloved disciple dared to say that "God is love." He has given the word "passion" a new meaning, for He has put a cross in the center of it. He alone has revealed a love, a passion, and a purity so magnetic and appealing that it has lifted millions out of the enslavement to lust. His love is the perfect illustration of the "expulsive power of a great affection."

Love, with the picture of Christ as its center, is the most beautiful thing in the universe. It longs to give and encourage, to lift and comfort, to share and save, to ennoble and transform; love longs to do this every day of our lives, without thought of rest and without consideration of self (F. pp. 30, 31).

From eternity Jesus has had an inveterate, incurable habit of creating and transforming. Because it is His nature to change bad to good, low to high, sorrow to joy, He loves us for our need and our imperfections . . .

We acquire this taste for lifting others by dwelling in Christ's company . . . One burning soul sets another on fire. Thus did the disciples learn from Jesus. "He chose twelve that they might be with Him," that they might listen and talk, work and rest, eat and sleep with Him for three years until in the end they began to be like Him. He transforms by intimate contact (F. pp. 28, 29).

CHRIST LIVETH IN ME

I am crucified with Christ: nevertheless I live; yet not I, but Christ liveth in me (Galatians 2:20).

How can Christ live in us? In what part of us? If our thoughts are flooded with Him, then He lives in our minds. We need no ghostly theory to prove that much; He is in our thoughts when we think about Him. He also lives in our wills if we yield them to Him. If he fills our thoughts and controls our wills, He will inevitably mold our acts. When He directs our acts, then He is master of our hands, feet, tongues and bodies. He does not force our wills. He comes in only where we open the doors of our hearts and give Him a cordial welcome. He waits until we say with our whole soul in utter sincerity:

Take my will and make it Thine;
It shall be no longer mine.

Take my heart, it is Thine own;
It shall be Thy royal throne! (F. p. 19)

When He enters, we change our business. We put *His* shingle up, and it is "The Kingdom of God." As His junior partner, my business is to offer my mind to Him, my hands to Him, every fiber of my body to Him, to work for His Kingdom (C. p. 20).

In our bodies today He continues to save the world, the task which He began as a Child in Bethlehem. We help Him with our witness and our lives. He knocks at other hearts. He stands at the door and knocks at every heart. The voice outside the other hearts with which He calls is *our voice* and *His* (C. p. 19).

Especially we may be sure to find Christ where there is distress, or poverty, or fear, or bereavement, or loneliness, or helplessness, or heartbreaks, or despair, or penitence. Watch for Him in a look of pain. Watch for Him in the beggars on the roadside. That is where He appeared in Lowell's *The Vision of Sir Launfal*. He is always drawn to the center of every need (F. pp. 21, 22).

CHRIST'S LOVE
CONSTRAINS US

For the love of Christ constraineth us (II Corinthians 5:14).

One of the chief functions of the religion of Jesus is to cut channels for love which will direct it into magnificent spiritual achievements...

The way to purify love and make it lift the soul constantly higher is to fall in love with Jesus, to lavish one's affections upon Him as Mary Magdalene lavished her affections upon Him when she knelt weeping at His feet and pouring costly perfumes on Him (F. p. 140).

If we do that it will not be necessary for us to worry about our character. If we keep "looking unto Jesus," the change will take place of itself. Our line of action is simple—forget ourselves, let go, focus our attention upon Jesus, and trust everything to Him. If we continue to admire Him and to imitate Him day by day, the change will take place inside us without introspection . . . (F. pp. 145, 146).

If we were perfectly Christlike we would search every face and look deep into every eye for signs of need that we could help. We would be enormously interested in people, and we would believe in them more than they believe in themselves . . . But all this Christlikeness comes to us as a direct result of friendship with Jesus . . .

Christ's friendship gives power. But this can be said only with strict reservations. Christ gives us power to carry out *His* purposes. He does not give us power to carry through our own schemes, those schemes which we had before we surrendered them all to Him.

This power He would give us only if we were safe with it! If Christ could trust us to use His power for wise and purely unselfish purposes, He would send it surging through us, not only willingly, but with tremendous eagerness (F. pp. 147, 148).

BECOMING
SONS OF GOD

As many as received him, to them
gave he power to become the sons of
God, even to them that believe on his
name (John 1:12).

Jesus has the same power today that He had in the days of
His flesh to enter the hearts of men and to drive out devils. This
is no new truth and it is no guess. It is one of the best attested
facts in the world. Millions of people of every race and continent
have felt His magnetic charm lift them out of sin and despair.
What He said about Himself is true: "I, if I be lifted up from
the earth, will draw all men unto me." That He has this mighty
lifting power each of us may easily prove for himself. To feel that
lift we need only touch Him as iron touches a magnet (F. p. 3).

In all human history there is nothing as relentless as the love
of Jesus—hard, like a diamond and as transparent. It *gives* all
and *demands* all. Thus Jesus is terrifyingly strict about sin. No
suggestion of evil can enter the holy of holies where He abides.
Jesus and sin are incompatible, cannot remain together. The sin
goes or He goes.

What about our sins of our past? The Master is eager to
cover them and to forget them, if we repent and cease to sin,
but He will neither forget nor forgive our *purpose* to do wrong
in the *future* . . . We cannot read books of which Jesus disap-
proves. Our conversation and even our very thoughts must
please Him. Our words must be honest. Our dealings must be
honest. Our work must be done as honestly as we can do it. He
will not tolerate poor work . . .

Jesus climaxes these uncompromising demands of His with

the final words: "Be ye therefore perfect, even as your Father which is in heaven is perfect." And He meant it! (F. pp. 58, 59).

If God has His way in each of us, our future is so dazzling that the imagination reels to contemplate it. Paul saw this, and he cried, "Eye has not seen nor ear heard, nor has it ever entered into the heart of man what God is preparing for those who love him (B. p. 26).

CHRISTIANITY IS CONCERN FOR OTHERS

I please all men in all things, not seeking mine own profit, but the profit of many, that they may be saved (I Corinthians 10:33).

The most tragic fact in the world is that so many people who have professed the Christian religion and joined Christian churches refuse to accept Christ's Way. They hear it, and agree that it is fine. But they do not practice it (G. p. 19).

Two things will continue to stand out high above all others. First, the unthinkable peril for the world. Second, the uncompromising demands of Jesus Christ to sacrifice self for the cause (B. p. 14).

Suppose Jesus had said: "I will not receive you into heaven at all unless you have done your best to bring everyone else to me." Would that not give us worry? Well, that is exactly what He meant when He said: "Inasmuch as ye did it not to one of the least of these, ye did it not to me."

We *for our age* stand where Jesus stood for His age—midway between God and lost men. It is a terrifying thought. We dare kick no one down. We must reach one hand up and one hand down as He did. "He that findeth his life shall lose it: and he that loseth his life for my sake shall find it."

The acid test of Christianity is what we do when we encounter unattractive or repulsive people. The natural man allows himself to be moved by winsome personalities; he is neutral or even antagonistic toward those who are without charm or appeal . . .

As the spirit of Jesus permeates us, we shall be enabled to conquer one antipathy after another until at last nothing can separate us from anyone . . . If Jesus were to speak to you He would say: "I love all the people you will meet today. I love them all and will not let them go. I am striving to be their Saviour and Friend. I am depending on you to help me" (F. pp. 76, 77, 81).

THE HOLY SPIRIT:
GOD WITHIN US

And I will pray the Father, and he shall give you another Comforter, that he may abide with you for ever; . . . for he dwelleth with you, and shall be in you (John 14:16, 17b).

God is, and always was, a Spirit— "the Holy Spirit." As a Spirit He came upon Mary and she conceived. When Jesus was baptized in the river Jordan He saw the Holy Spirit come upon Him as a dove . . .

After His crucifixion Christ arose with a supernatural body, having power to appear or disappear at will . . . Just before His departure He said He would return. For ten days after His ascension the disciples assembled together in Jerusalem daily for prayer and praise, waiting for the promise to be fulfilled.

Then on the day of Pentecost there came a mighty blast like a wind, which filled their house, and brought thousands of people in Jerusalem running to see what was happening. Flames of fire came and separated and stood on every head, and "they were all filled with the Holy Spirit." Christ had returned as pure Spirit so that He might live in *them* and in us, and in "as many as would receive him."

In many a Pentecost since that day He has come with just such tremendous power to dwell in people who were ready to receive Him . . . God, the Maker of the Worlds—God, who took for Himself a human form—God, who comes into us as Holy Spirit, is "the same God, yesterday, today, and forever" (F. pp. 167, 168).

The Father pours the Spirit out through Jesus, then through His disciples out to others and on and on through the world. On the first Pentecost day the Spirit reached three thousand people.

So today you and I have only one responsibility. We must go forth with the floodgates wide open upward and wide open outward and let the rivers of living water flow from God to men (B. p. 137).

"Have ye received the Holy Ghost, since ye believed?" (Acts 19:2).

THE DOORWAY TO
THE DIVINE INFLOWING

Yield yourselves unto God, as those
that are alive from the dead, and
your members as instruments of righteousness unto God (Romans 6:13b).

Jesus said: "He that wills to do his will shall know . . ." Only experience can prove to the soul how surrender is the immediate doorway to the divine inflowing. The moment we surrender, we are deluged with God. That is the proof that Christ does keep knocking until we open the door, but He does not come in until we say with total sincerity: "I surrender all: all to Thee, my blessed Saviour, I surrender all" (C. p. 26).

We who have tried this find that when our surrender is perfect, without holding a single corner of ourselves away from Him, He enters and fills us with an astonishing sweetness. He calls us by names as intimate as "beloved," and the intimacy we have with Him, when the surrender is perfect, is the sweetest experience any human being ever enjoys . . .

To the surrendered soul He is a lover so beautiful that all other loves are nothing. Paul was speaking from his heart when he said: I count everything in the world as loss for the greatest gain of all—the gain of having Christ Jesus my Lord. For His sake I have lost everything and count it as waste to be thrown away so that I may have Christ and be with Him (Philippians 3:7, 8) (C. p. 25).

There is nothing we need to do but keep repeating over and over and over and over . . . "This house is all yours, Lord. What next?" That seems to make us perfect conductors, like pure

46

copper wire. That willingness of surrender to Him opens the channel, clears the wire, and He does His perfect will...

This is not something to play with at odd moments, but to work at assiduously, day after day, until it becomes such a fixed habit that it requires little or no effort to recall it, *every time we close our eyelids,* every time we think (C. pp. 23, 24).

HOW TO BE SURE CHRIST LIVES

> I know whom I have believed, and am persuaded that he is able to keep that which I have committed unto him against that day (II Timothy 1: 12b).

Jesus is alive, an invisible Person, more alive than you and I are. This is the reason why He can be—and pleads with us to allow Him to be—our friend now (F. p. 13).

This, I believe, is the crucial fact on which the fate of Christianity depends. If Christ did not rise from the dead He was a deluded idealist, mistaken at the point of His most vital belief, and the validity of all His other contentions would be open to doubt. Real friendship with Him would be impossible, at least for most of us (F. p. 12).

Because Christ is alive and here, a wonderfully intimate friendship is possible for us now. At this very moment I have that delightful experience of His friendship as I write. You may have it as you read. Indeed to millions of us there have come such intimate and wonderful visitations that we venture to tell them to those only who are able to appreciate them. All over the world the glories of Pentecost appear and reappear. We could not have these if Jesus were only a memory of one who died two thousand years ago (F. p. 16).

One of the most famous philosophers of religion will pardon me, I hope, if I quote what he said sadly to me: "I would give anything in the world to have the experience of Christ that you have." Speaking from the depths of my heart I gave him the only possible answer. "You will never find it along the pathway of pure intellect," I said, "It is revealed unto babes" (F. p. 17).

I had a personal experience of Christ in Mindanao, Philippine Islands, which left me sure that He not only lives, but lives in my heart. When He entered my heart, He brought to me a tender compassion for the multitudes which has been the driving power of my life ever since. The living Christ put it there (B. p. 23).

THE GREAT
REVIVAL

O Lord, revive thy work in the midst of the years, in the midst of the years make known; in wrath remember mercy (Habakkuk 3:2).

History will record that from 1950 onward America began to have her greatest religious revival. There is reason to hope that this is the beginning of the greatest revival of all time, not only in the United States, but throughout the whole world . . .

But this American revival is not confined to a few preachers or even to a few hundred preachers. Preaching is not the *cause* of this revival; the preachers whose churches are crowded have merely responded to the real cause . . .

The scientists started this revival, not with sermons, but with atom and hydrogen bombs and guided missiles. Newspapers and magazines have stimulated it to the point where they have Americans thoroughly scared about a future war that can destroy every human being in any large city in the world in a matter of seconds . . .

The popular preachers seldom mention war or bombs; that is the last thing people want to hear in church. They want sermons on "How to get rid of fear and worry," "How to emphasize the positive and eliminate the negative . . ."

This is of tremendous value, but it has one defect. The bomb and the threat still remain, while the "spiritual" tonic wears off in the course of a week. . .

This bomb hanging over our heads is producing another type of revival among thousands of people. When they turn to God they seem to hear Him say: "You ask *me* to save the world from catastrophe. I need *your* help! . . ."

The best measure of the power of this revival lies in determining how many men and women answer "Yes" to this call of God, and how many are willing to sacrifice their own plans and interests in order to help. Jesus called on His disciples to take up their cross and follow Him (B. pp. 11, 12, 13).

CHRIST IS
THE ANSWER

In him dwelleth all the fulness of the Godhead bodily. And ye are complete in him (Colossians 2:9, 10a).

Modern psychology bears out every word Jesus said about thoughts, with sledge-hammer emphasis. Every man's thinking takes on world-wide importance. *Every* evil thought not only contaminates the man himself, but makes the world worse, pushes it toward hell. Every good thought not only blesses the man himself but also pushes the entire world up toward heaven . . .

Several times Jesus repeated these words: "A good man out of the good treasure of his heart bringeth forth good things; and an evil man out of the evil *treasure* bringeth forth evil things."

A clean mind is good but not good enough.

It isn't enough to cleanse the mind of evil thoughts, though that is essential. An empty mind will not stay empty, or clean!

Moreover, a clean empty mind is purely negative and useless to others. It does nothing to fight or cancel out the active burning hate-thoughts which curse the world . . .

Fortunately, the knowledge that can save the world is already ours. It is the way of Jesus Christ, what He is, what He teaches, and how He transforms men . . .

But how shall we help all men to know Him? That was Paul's question, and it still is ours. The greatest way to help Christ conquer the world is to saturate our own minds with Him. We do this by thinking about Christ and His Kingdom *as much as we can* . . .

How can we saturate our minds with Christ? There is but one way to get a true picture of Him. This is to read His life in the four gospels so often that we know it by heart. We who wish to be Christlike ought never to allow a day to pass without reading at least a chapter of the gospels (E. pp. 70, 71, 72, 73, 74).

MIRACLE WORKING
CHRISTIANS

> He that believeth on me, the works
> that I do shall he do also; and greater
> works than these shall he do; because
> I go unto my Father (John 14:12).

We do not seem to be making many *miracle working Christians*
like Sadhu Sundar Singh. We preach and practice a weak Christianity (A. p. 16).

One of the chief functions of the religion of Jesus is to cut
channels for love which will direct it into magnificent spiritual
achievements (F. p. 140).

Everything Jesus said proves that He expected His disciples
to do "greater things" than He did. He expected all His miracles
to be possible for them and more. Whatever they asked in His
name, He declared, they should have if they were abiding in
Him. "Ask, and it shall be given you." Have faith, He told them,
and mountains will melt away.

This power He would give us only if we were safe with it! If
Christ could trust us to use His power for wise and purely
unselfish purposes, He would send it surging through us, not
only willingly, but with tremendous eagerness. Christ needs
powerful men today who will never use their power for self ...

But, when saintly men catch from Jesus the spirit of selfless
complete love, there comes an ever-rising power. Wonderful
people scattered here and there around the world are living
embodiments of this immense soul force now. Some heal
physical diseases, some diseases of the soul, and some diseases

of society. They whisper their questions to their unseen Companion, and He tells them what to do . . .

We need look no further for the secret of power. Jesus has told us clearly and repeatedly that His secret is *perfect obedience always*. And until we have tried that, we do not, of course, know what power can pour through us like an electric arc light melting steel! (F. pp. 147, 148, 149).

PRACTICING
THE PRESENCE

Lo, I am with you alway, even unto the end of the world (Matthew 28: 20b). I will never leave thee, nor forsake thee (Hebrew 13:5b).

At last God gets so close that one stops thinking of God as outside himself, and begins to think of Christ inside in one's own thought and breast. He sees God's thoughts flow into his mind. Sometimes one feels that they are coming in from above but more often one feels that these thoughts are welling up from the unconscious, as from a hidden fountain. God is so close then that He not only lives around us, but all through us. And this is exactly the way God wants it to be . . .

The rewards are beyond description. In the first place, perpetual prayer produces an immense change in the way we think . . . instead of telling God what we want from Him, we ask Him what He wants *us* to do (B. pp. 96, 97).

The moment I allow myself to cut loose from Thee, O Christ of God, I become despicable and my will divides against itself. When my will clings to Thy will, miracles happen. I have seen miracles happening . . . Thou art the vine; this branch and these millions of branches wither except when we abide in Thee.

52

Deeper yet, O Christ, deeper, deeper, yet into Thy broken heart let me bury my will, that from Thy heart I may draw the power of Pentecost. Help me *stay*. Help me *abide*. Nothing else in the world matters but that: the power to stay deep in Thy broken heart (A. p. 30).

FRIENDSHIP WITH JESUS

I have called you friends; for all things that I have heard of my Father I have made known unto you (John 15:15b). Ye are my friends, if . . . (John 15:14).

Emerson says, in his famous essay on *Friendship,* that ideal friendships require "natures so rare and costly, so well tempered and so happily adapted to one another" that very seldom can this high level of intimacy be attained. Each party to friendship must pay the supreme price. Each must give to the other the best he has. Perfect friendship is as beautiful and as delicate as a rose. If there be treachery, suspicion, selfishness, irritability, callousness, vulgarity, or low aim in the relationship, perfect friendship is impossible.

If this be true, we may well ask: What high price must be paid for the friendship of Jesus? Jesus Himself gave the answer with breathtaking directness: "Ye are my friends, *if ye do whatsoever I command.*" Nothing could be clearer or more final. Surrender, absolute, eager, and continuous, is the price . . .

When Jesus demands us to do "whatsoever I command," He is not more absolute than Nature herself. "Obey or perish" is written into the warp and woof of the universe. Nature's laws, which are God's laws, are never broken, the men who fail to obey them are broken. The horrors of our age are the result of the failure of men to apply the Sermon on the Mount to nations and individuals ... Christ is no temporary or passing acquaintance, but a friend for eternity ... Christ offers his Blood bond of Saviour, Friend, Master for eternity. That or nothing! That *high* or nothing! That is why the requirements of his friendship are so lofty, because the stakes are so tremendous (F. pp. 55, 56, 57).

Although it is true that Christ requires total obedience, yet this obedience turns out, as Paul told the people of Galatia, to be perfect freedom. Indeed eager, glad obedience to duty is the only real liberty in this universe (F. p. 138).

MAKING OUR WORLD A PARADISE

> The earth shall be full of the knowledge of the LORD, as the waters cover the sea (Isaiah 11:9b).

We can make a paradise out of our whole world any time we choose. We have the scientific knowledge; we need make no new discoveries. There is more than enough genius in production, an abundance of raw materials and more manpower than we know what to do with. More than enough of everything to build a paradise! Of everything save—love. We need only live the command of Jesus "Love thy neighbor as thyself" and all of us within thirty years shall have ample. This does not refer to a few favored countries but to the entire planet. Indeed it is impossible for a few favored countries alone to have plenty. What we have we must share (F. p. 1).

Jesus has the same power today that He had in the days of

His flesh to enter the hearts of men and to drive out devils. This is no new truth and it is no guess. It is one of the best attested facts in the world. Millions of people of every race and continent have felt His magnetic charm lift them out of sin and despair. What He said about Himself is true: "I, if I be lifted up from the earth, will draw all men unto me." That He has this mighty lifting power each of us may easily prove for himself. To feel that lift we need only touch Him as iron touches a magnet (F. p. 3).

Volumes could be written, and have been written, about the compassion of Christ within the Christian Church; that is to be expected. The Church ceases to be the Church when the compassion of Christ does not flow through it (G. p. 5).

The only hope for this evil, selfish world is for the living Christ to abide in enough of us to change the spiritual climate of the world. He alone is able to change greed to compassion, fear to faith, and hate to love (B. p. 23).

Only prayer, which releases the infinite might of God, can win this final battle for men's minds and hearts—this battle against hate, this battle for "one world" (E. p. 11).

TURN ON
LOVE

Owe no man anything, but to love one another: for he that loveth another hath fulfilled the law (Romans 13:8).

We could make the whole world right if we joined in an all-out crusade for the way of Christ.

But before we can change the world like that, we American Christians must first change ourselves. We are sixty per cent sham in our following of Jesus today. That is all too easy to prove. Christ told us, "Love your neighbor as yourself." He did that. If *we* did it, we could save the world. But we are counterfeit Christians. We do not love our competitors in business as we love ourselves. Or do we? Still less do we love the people of other countries as we love our own people. The very idea of doing that sounds unpatriotic—or like a violation of our Constitution! But until we do love our neighbor-nations as we love ourselves, we can neither win them as friends nor change their ways.

We must prove that love with unselfish deeds. Communism began because the masses of Russia were in poverty and the Communists promised to give them something better. Communism breeds today wherever people are hungry and dissatisfied. Who will deny that? About fifteen hundred million people, two thirds of the world, who are hungry and unhappy today hear the promises of the Communists, and they will go communist unless they are assured that we will help them out of their misery.

The answer to the promises of the Communists is clear; it is to go with a compassionate program of helping needy people to help themselves, and so prove that we are their friends. If we did enough of that we could make those fifteen hundred millions our firm friends. We could win even Russia and China back to our friendship (B. p. 16).

Loving service is our way out—not fear and fierce threats. As Rufus Moseley used to say: "If your love has not yet worked, *turn on more love!*" "Perfect love casteth out fear" when it is shown in deeds and not merely in pretense. When we all put our shoulders under this magnificent cause of a world of abundance, there soon will be no one to fear (G. p. 244).

WORLD VISION

The gospel of the kingdom shall be preached in all the world for a witness unto all nations; and then shall the end come (Matthew 24:14).

The most acute need of our age is for global-minded people who "Think the world thought, do the world deed, and pray the world prayer" (E. p. 86).

Some readers of this book may be murmuring: "There is scarcely a word about what prayer and right thinking will do for *me*! It is all about what I can do for others." That omission was deliberate. There are enough books already on helping yourself through prayer—on how to get what you want, how to acquire riches, how to find health, how to be famous, how to go to heaven. But in this era, when our bleeding world faces the worst crisis in history, when it calls like a drowning man, it is contemptibly selfish to ask what advantage will come to us if we go to her rescue.

Nevertheless, this much may be said. The habit of praying for others makes you noble.

Your thoughts grow wider and higher,

Your selfishness melts away.

You become Christlike.

You bless mankind.

You are loved by all who know you.

People think you are beautiful, for

You become radiant with the smile of Christ.

Your joy comes from what you give, not from what you accumulate (E. pp. 93, 94).

Your contribution can be titanic beyond all imagination. It depends upon one thing only—how much *time* and *heart* and *mind* and *soul* and *strength* and *prayer* and give to *God's world task* (E. p. 95).

THE HIGHEST
COMPASSION

The Spirit of the LORD is upon me, because he hath anointed me to preach the gospel to the poor; he hath sent me to heal the broken-hearted, to preach deliverance to the captives, and recovering of sight to the blind, to set at liberty them that are bruised (Luke 4:18).

Open the pages of the gospels and you find Jesus spending all His time every day, all day, lifting people out of their misery and sin. Every minute of His waking hours was devoted to healing and helping and feeding and saving, except when He retreated to solitary prayer to renew His strength.

What no one else did at all for the multitudes before, He did all the time.

His life is perfectly described in the song:

> Jesus, Thou art all compassion,
> Pure, unbounded love Thou art.

The compassion of Jesus was indeed unbounded. Any stranger of any faith or race in need anywhere called forth His compassion and His help. He did not stop with feeling sorry. He did the thing each man needed most. He healed the lepers. He opened the eyes of the blind. He fed the hungry. He never threw a coin to a beggar! He healed him of his disease or blindness, so that he no longer needed to beg. He healed twisted minds and sinsick souls. He always finished His job before He left the person who had been in trouble, so that the healed man could help himself.

Jesus was the first man in all history who devoted His entire life to *permanent* cures. He could not tolerate halfway measures. He completely healed body, mind, and soul . . .

He declared that God does not want men to be the way they are, in destitution or oppression or despair or sin. "All things are possible," He said, "to him that believeth" (G. pp. 26, 27).

WE LOVE A PERSON MORE THAN AN ABSTRACTION

We love him, because he first loved us (I John 4:19).

If, therefore, we wish the world to adopt the principles of Jesus, we must help the world to fall in love with Him.

Most of us find that codes of ethics, or beautiful mottoes, or firm resolves have little more power to hold us than if we clung to a cloud. In this respect Paul was one of us. He tried to obey the Jewish law, but it did not have enough holding power to keep him from falling. He cried, "I do not do the good things that I want to do."

But when Paul surrendered his heart to Jesus Christ he found what has been called the "expulsive power of a great affection." His tremendous love for Christ took away all taste for the evils he had previously liked. "I count all things but loss for the excellency of the knowledge of Christ Jesus my Lord; for whom

I have suffered the loss of all things, and do count them rubbish that I may win Christ."

Jesus has the same power today that He had in the days of His flesh to enter the hearts of men and to drive out devils. This is no new truth and it is no guess. It is one of the best attested facts in the world. Millions of people of every race and continent have felt His magnetic charm lift them out of sin and despair. What He said about Himself is true: "I, if I be lifted up from the earth, will draw all men unto me." That He has this mighty lifting power each of us may easily prove for himself. To feel that lift we need only touch Him as iron touches a magnet (F. p. 2, 3).

When Christ lives in me, life is exciting. He is powerful beyond words or limits— He can do anything, change anything, stop anything. Not, we must remember, at our bidding, but when *He* desires. We are in partnership with a miracle Worker! He loves variety and beauty—look at the flowers! and listen to great music! (C. p. 36).

PRAYER THAT MOVES MOUNTAINS

Jesus said unto them . . . If ye have faith as a grain of mustard seed, ye shall say unto this mountain, Remove hence to yonder place; and it shall remove; and nothing shall be impossible unto you (Matthew 17:20).

Right praying, Jesus repeatedly declared, can remove mountains, can accomplish anything. Before this last war many people had regarded His sweeping statements as "Oriental exaggeration," or at least not true of our day. But people are changing their minds. There is a strong and widespread swing back toward faith in the might of prayer (E. p. 11).

"Prayer alone will not be enough," you say. "We need right deeds." Precisely! But prayer is the door that opens our minds and the minds of our leaders to God, so that we and they may know what deeds are right . . .

We do not "persuade God to try harder" when we pray; it is our world leaders, our statesmen and church men whom we persuade to try harder. We help God when we pray. When great numbers of us pray for leaders, a mighty invisible spiritual force lifts its minds and eyes toward God. His Spirit flows through our prayer to them, and He can speak to them directly (E. pp. 14, 15).

We who are Christian hold the world's fate in our hands, for whether the rest of the world learns the secret of Jesus or not depends on us. We cannot evade this; God challenges you and me to help our age push its spiritual knowledge beyond where it is at the moment (B. p. 123).

THE POWER
OF SILENCE

In quietness and in confidence shall
be your strength: (Isaiah 30:15b).

Prayer is likely to be undervalued by all but wise people because it is so silent and so secret. We are often deceived into thinking that noise is more important than silence. War sounds far more important than the noiseless growing of a crop of wheat, yet the silent wheat feeds millions, while war destroys

61

them. No one but God knows how often prayers have changed the course of history. Many a man who prayed received no credit excepting in heaven. We are tempted to turn from prayer to something more noisy like speeches or guns, because our motives are mixed. We are interested in the making of a better world, of course, but we also want people to know what we have done.

Secret prayer for others all during the day is an acid test of our unselfishness. Our little selves must fade out, leaving a self-forgetting channel, through which God's warmth flows unhindered in lovely unending prayer. The highest form of communion is not asking God for things for ourselves, but letting Him flow down through us, out over the world in endless benediction (E. p. 24).

To hear God we must do two things, not just one. The first is to spend our days with our attention and our interest fastened on things that are good . . .

Our minds are beaten and wounded by the pitiless sounds and sights that crowd in from the outside world. We are defeated, terribly defeated by our own world. The radio, the noises that swirl about us, our social engagements, our work, all crowd out our own thinking, crowd out any chance of listening to our own deeper, subconscious mind. That is why the Quakers are very wise when they go to their meeting-houses and sit in complete silence for an hour every week. Moral Rearmament varies this by listening in silence with pencil in hand.

It is difficult to become calm and receptive to God. But the more difficult it is, the more necessary it is for us to discipline ourselves (B. p. 146).

CHRIST
IMPARTS POWER

Behold, I give unto you power to tread on serpents and scorpions, and over all the power of the enemy: and nothing shall by any means hurt you (Luke 10:19).

Christ is not only the most *powerful* Person the world has known; He is the noblest. All the highest ideals since His day, as H. G. Wells declares, have sprung from His teachings. What is more, Jesus Himself lived His ideals even better than He could find words to express them. Nine tenths of the human race would follow Christ, if they knew what He is, when they would not follow an abstract truth.

But how shall we help all men to know Him? That was Paul's question, and it still is ours. The greatest way to help Christ conquer the world is to saturate our own minds with Him. We do this by thinking about Christ and His Kingdom *as much as we can.* If we think about Him we shall inevitably witness for Him and work for Him.

Other people will catch Him from us by our deeds and words. "Out of the fullness of the heart the mouth speaketh."

How can we saturate our minds with Christ? There is but one way to get a true picture of Him. This is to read His life in the four gospels so often that we know it by heart. We who wish to be Christlike ought never to allow a day to pass without reading at least a chapter of the gospels (E. pp. 73, 74).

NEW HOPE
FOR THE MULTITUDES

The angel said unto them, Fear not:
for, behold, I bring you good tidings
of great joy, which shall be to all
people (Luke 2:10).

When compassion for the common man was born on Christmas Day, with it was born new hope among the multitudes. They feel a great, ever-rising determination to lift themselves and their children out of hunger and disease and misery, up to a higher level. Jesus started a fire upon the earth, and it is burning hot today. The fire of a new hope is in the hearts of the hungry multitudes . . .

Now we are beginning to realize that the Lord's Prayer is for everyone in the whole world. The "O" which begins that prayer is as big as the earth! It ought to be renamed: "The Lord's World-Prayer."

"Our Father" is the prayer that God will be the Father of all races and of all lands— "Thy will be done on earth."

"Our daily bread" means enough bread for every last child in both the Eastern and Western hemispheres.

"As we forgive those who trespass against us" means as we forgive *all* nations in the whole wide world.

"Thy Kingdom come . . . on earth" means *all* the earth.

All this God wanted before we asked Him. Then why pray it? We are beginning to see dimly that the Lord's Prayer is not a *request* for God to give us things; it is an enlistment. God has always wanted everything in that prayer to happen. It is we

64

who need to change, not God. This prayer, all of it, actually is a dedication of ourselves to helping His will be done, His Kingdom to come, His people to be fed in every corner of the earth. This is prayer at its highest, for it is not asking God to shrivel down to our small purposes. It is trying to stretch our hearts to the size of His world plans (G. pp. 30, 31).

YOU CAN BE
FULL OF CHRIST

For in him (Christ) dwelleth all the fulness of the Godhead bodily. And ye are complete in him (Colossians 2:9, 10a).

Thank God, one needs no unusual ability to be full of Christ, one need not profess unusual goodness, nor worthiness, nor an unusual past, nor blue blood, nor social connections, nor money. The Gospel is for everyone, and "no questions asked."

Listen and say, "Yes." Enter God's open door unafraid. He is there waiting. Down God's street there are always green lights. What an undefeatable Gospel!

A friend remonstrated, "You make it altogether too easy. This is the hardest achievement on earth and your light-hearted promises will deceive people."

Very well, then, let us say plainly it *does cost*. You have got to *stop loving things and yourself*. There is no substitute for that. Worshiping mammon and self is of all ways of living the most wretched. Let go courageously of *self* and *things*, and, lo! it is as easy to begin living with Him as breathing. The final goal is far,

far away, but every step with Him toward that goal is heavenly! (E. p. 84).

We must not underestimate the time required to become proficient, or we may say impatiently, "It can't be done," which is sheer nonsense. It can't be done *well* in a day. It can't be learned *perfectly* in a year. But it can become nearly perfect in ten years. Meanwhile, the progress from day to day is so thrilling, and the satisfactions so wonderful, that every day is a joy. Perhaps we do other people more good while we are still learners than after we have become perfect, for we understand their difficulties and they understand ours. "The best teacher is he who is also a learner."

Even after a lifetime of prayer, the saints realize that they do not fully attain the perfect surrender of Christ to the thought of God. There will always be heights for us to attain—and that adds to the zest of living (E. p. 78).

WHERE CAN
I FIND GOD?

He that hath seen me hath seen the Father; and how sayest thou *then,* Shew us the Father? (John 14:9b).

Someone may ask, "Where can I find God?" Our answer is the answer Jesus gave: "He that hath seen me hath seen the Father . . . No man cometh unto the Father, but by me."

I used to deny this. "Surely," I thought, "multitudes of non-Christians know God." Yes, they know God, but not "the Father of Jesus Christ," not this Father with the intense fire of love coursing hotter than the sun. *This* Father is found only through Jesus.

Christ revealed that side of God's nature, the side which neither science nor history could reveal—God's tenderness, His sympathetic sweetness. Jesus alone was able to reveal "love so amazing, so divine," surpassing everything the world ever supposed possible. The Bible strains at words to help us appreciate this "Father of our Lord Jesus Christ . . . that ye may be able to comprehend . . . what is the breadth, and length, and depth, and height; and to know the love of Christ, which passeth knowledge, that ye might be filled with all the fulness of God." Words of inconceivable love.

Jesus is so lovable that masses of men would be won to His Love if He could be shown to them clearly *as love* (F. p. 37).

The person of Christ not only transforms us and our conception of other human beings, but it transforms our idea of God. Through Jesus we see a very intimate and understandable and approachable and magnetic God (F. p. 36).

WE CAN!
ENOUGH OF US CAN!

I can do all things through Christ which strengtheneth me (Philippians 4:13).

We can! We don't need to wait! It's in our power now! We can have a world of peace, justice, happiness, the kingdom of God as soon as we want it. Every new scientific discovery can bend to aid humanity if people will love Christ and one another. But we must pay a price, just as soldiers must give up all they cherish. We must give up most of our ordinary little thinking for the world's sake.

Non-Christians do not constitute more than half of God's problem. Christians who sit on the side lines and do not help, are the other half of His problem. It isn't that they can't, it isn't that they won't, it is just that they *don't,* because they *don't know we can.* Many more of us would "get into the game" if we saw how *important, how terrifyingly* important each of us is for the saving of our generation; if we saw how easy it would be for us to help tip the scales toward the kingdom of God; if we saw that *all the time, no matter where we are,* right thinking builds a bridge between God and other men—the bridge that God *needs* if His will is to be done on earth and if this generation is to be saved from destroying itself.

We have enough Christian people to transform the world right now, if only their thoughts were always on Christ's side. But they suppose their thoughts are their own, and so a large part of their thinking cancels out the rest of their thinking ...

We need to mobilize the minds of the men of good will so that they will form a mighty *mass attack of good thoughts.* Then we all together will tip the scales the other way, will lift the world upward to a new high, in spite of the selfish little thoughts of mean people ...

Here is a principle most people need:

Fix your thoughts upon what ought to come to pass, and not upon the things you dislike. Let the things we oppose die of neglect. For we help everything we think about—even when we are thinking against it! (E. pp. 92, 93).

THE TRANSFORMING
FRIENDSHIP

I call you not servants; for the
servant knoweth not what his lord
doeth: but I have called you friends;
for all things that I have heard of
my Father I have made known unto
you (John 15:15).

The friendship of Jesus opens into new continents of glorious
experience. We often hear people say that they could do
wonderful things if only they were differently situated. But the
most precious gift in the world is ours anywhere. We do not
need any different situation to enjoy Jesus. For example, nearly
everyone can take a walk alone. That walk is pregnant with
infinite possibilities which are at one's very elbow. Some of us
always walk on the right side of the sidewalk so that Jesus can
walk unseen on our left side. We talk to Him about the people
who are passing. The following conversation with Jesus actually
took place on the street:

"I am so glad, dear Christ, that you are unseen by my side. I
can see You with my mind's eye, turning Your face toward me,
putting Your arm around me. The other people would be
surprised if they saw You that way. They would wonder who
You are, wouldn't they, Master?"

"What can we do, Master, together, for these people that we
meet? What can I do, Lord, to help You, as I go by?"

"You can look into their eyes with love and think of Me as
you look. Your thought will be like a rebroadcasting station and
will help them to open their minds to my spirit. When they look
at you, they attune themselves to you, although they are not

aware of Me. So I reach them through you. That is how each of us helps the other. In such mutual aid our friendship grows closer" (F. pp. 48, 49).

HOW TO FIND
CHRIST BY YOUR SIDE

> I was an hungred, and ye gave me meat: I was thirsty, and ye gave me drink: I was a stranger, and ye took me in: Naked, and ye clothed me: I was sick, and ye visited me: I was in prison, and ye came unto me (Matthew 25:35, 36).

Let us go out and help some needy person, and suddenly we shall find Christ by our side, because we have caught up with Him.

If we perform some act of kindness, it is often astonishing how quickly the sense of joy and of assurance that He is with us begins to flood our hearts.

1. Visit a sick person and pray by his bedside . . .
2. Try to pray with the poorest people in the slums of your city and to help them until it hurts your pocketbook . . .
3. Go to a prison. Listen to the stories of prisoners, comfort or help them, and tell them the love of Christ . . .
4. Select an article of clothing which you value highly and give it to some needy person who cannot repay you . . .
5. Comfort someone who has just lost a loved one . . .
6. Sacrifice all the plans that you have cherished for a successful life, and yield yourself to the cause of bringing Christ into men's lives . . .
7. If you are seated in a crowded bus, offer your seat to a woman, or to an old person, or to one weaker than yourself . . .
8. Go out of your way to greet strangers . . . and help them . . .

9. Give yourself unhurriedly to be helpful to a child, in some matter which seems important to him . . .

Better than books or sermons these experiments demonstrate that there is profound truth in the twenty-fifth chapter of Matthew: "Insofar as you did it to one of the humblest of these brothers of mine, you did it to me" (F. pp. 89, 90, 91).

THINK CHRIST'S THOUGHTS

Let this mind be in you, which was also in Christ Jesus (Philippians 2:5).

Thinking about Christ constantly is easy to understand. It is not easy to do. Yet there is a way to do it without stopping our other occupations. It is to acquire a new way of thinking. Thinking is a process of talking to your "inner self." Instead of talking to yourself, talk to the Invisible Christ. If you do that all day every day, then your thoughts are spreading Christ all over the planet wherever other minds are turned into yours. Hundreds of thousands, or perhaps millions, of minds will be better . . .

Thought transformed into conversation with Christ becomes larger, more unselfish, more worthwhile, cleaner, more noble. Try it . . .

The universe pays the price if you and I fail to measure up to our highest!

The sheer responsibility of this realization might drive one mad if it were not for the one redeeming fact that by the help of Christ *we can* think His thoughts. When we share our thoughts with Him, the enormous responsibility for the future of the world rolls over on His shoulders. He carries what is too big for us, and He supplies the power. Paul's marvelous words, as translated by Goodspeed, are true: "God working through us is able to do unutterably more" (E. pp. 76, 77, 91).

When you think in perfect harmony with God, the titanic forces of the universe bend like gravity to pull things and people your direction, because you are going in God's direction. One man with God shall be stronger than ten thousand! (E. p. 91).

FOLLOW FIRST: KNOW LATER

If any man will do his will, he shall know of the doctrine, whether it be of God, or *whether* I speak of myself (John 7:17).

You may ask, "How much must I believe about Jesus in order to try cultivating His friendship?" All you need do is to agree that He is worth following; and then you follow, just as the disciples did. Consider how little they knew about Jesus at the beginning; they knew far less than we know. They saw an interesting and magnetic personality; they decided to walk with Him and see what He would do. After they had followed Him for a few months their hearts felt a tremendous love and their minds reached a tremendous truth . . .

What most men think they know about Jesus is half mistaken, because they have not carefully studied His life story. We must watch Him walking across the pages of the New Testament. We must ask Him what interested Him most and what were the things which He rejected. This is no short task though it is a happy one. We find that even after we have practically memorized all Jesus ever did or said, new flashes of insight keep coming at every new reading.

As we become better acquainted with Him we see that He was primarily interested in people and in their problems. He was passionately fond of helping those in need. He saw deep needs that others failed to see. He was called the greatest Physician because He healed everything and everyone He touched. He could not endure seeing men suffer. As you read in the gospel of Mark of His cures, piling high upon one another, you feel there was in Him a love hot enough to burn out disease. To this day people healed in the name of Jesus—and there are many of them—say they feel a warm glow pass through their bodies when the disease goes. His love literally burns out disease (F. pp. 4, 5, 6).

HOW TO KEEP
THE MIND PURE

Keep thy heart with all diligence;
for out of it are the issues of life
(Proverbs 4:23).

How shall we keep the germs of evil out of our minds? The well-known laws of association offer an answer. Every memory is tied to many other ideas, so that if one of these associated ideas comes to the surface of consciousness it tries to drag the others into the consciousness with it. If we have ever seen a tree struck by lightning, the sight of that tree in the future is quite certain to bring to mind the lightning, the clap of thunder, and our own fright. The sight of a bad picture evokes in the mind a whole train of thoughts we would be ashamed to confess to our mothers.

On the other hand, a picture of Christ, or a sentence from the Bible, is likely to flood the mind with pure and lovely memories which we have previously associated with Him. Every time we read our Bibles or think of Christ, we make this great storehouse of beautiful ideas richer. It is one way in which we "lay up treasures in heaven." To keep our thought-stream pure all the time, we must hold Christ before the eye and ear as often as possible. There is nothing magic or ghostly or mysterious about this. It is simply applied psychology.

If we place pictures of Christ where we will see them as we open our eyes in the morning, if we read some of His story in the gospels, we shall start our day with clean thoughts. If we plan our offices and dining rooms and living rooms so that our eyes will catch the eyes of Christ, or see such mottoes as "Think Thy thoughts in my mind," we shall be able to bring our minds back to their best and the whole day will be enriched by beautiful ideas (F. pp. 70, 71).

CHANNELS OF GOD'S POWER

It is God which worketh in you both to will and to do of *his* good pleasure (Philippians 2:13).

Many people who have opened themselves toward God have had a marvelous experience for a few minutes or a few hours, but because the pipe was closed at the bottom the spirit's flow came to a stop, and they wondered what was the matter. That has been the experience of many Christian people ever since Christ came. They have opened, they have received a great blessing, and then their Christian life has come to a standstill, and they wondered why! Their little bucket could hold only a small amount, and it was soon full. The infinite resources of heaven were awaiting them; all they had to do was to open the gate at the bottom—to kick the bottom out of their buckets—and to let God flow through. It doesn't matter how big heaven is; it matters how big our pipe is and whether it is open. The bottleneck is never God; it is always ourselves.

In one respect, however, we are different from a pipe. A pipe cannot decide how big it will be, and we can. We can grow. We are small pipes at first, but if we keep open all the time the total flow for a day and a month will be great and, as the flow continues, we will become bigger pipes . . .

We become channels like that simply by being willing and unselfish. But the moment we desire to keep any of the power for ourselves we cease to flow. If we strut and say, "Look at me," as the spirit passes through, that "me" obstructs the passage. The Spirit of God doesn't flow until the "me" is washed out and only the pipe line is left . . .

Stop being a terminus and become a bridge! Stop being a bucket and become a pipe! That is the secret of receiving the power of God (B. 55, 56).

GIVING AWAY,
WE KEEP

Is not this the fast that I have chosen? to loose the bands of wickedness, to undo the heavy burdens, and to let the oppressed go free, and that ye break every yoke?

Is it not to deal thy bread to the hungry, and that thou bring the poor that are cast out to thy house? when thou seest the naked, that thou cover him; and that thou hide not thyself from thine own flesh?

Then shall thy light break forth as the morning, and thine health shall spring forth speedily: and thy righteousness shall go before thee; the glory of the LORD shall be thy rereward (Isaiah 58:6-8).

Many people tell us of sharp disappointment soon after they have had a great spiritual experience. This happens after revival meetings so often that some people are bitterly opposed to all revivals. They say that the reaction is bad.

The trouble is not with the revival, but with something else. I believe it is because our bucket is filled up, and there is no room for more. We begin to coast along on the memory of a wonderful experience, and it turns bad, like manna in the wilderness or like milk left in a pail.

The spirit of God is like gasoline in a tank of an automobile or an airplane. It is of no use unless it is harnessed to accomplish something. If you have had a spiritual experience and it is slipping from your grasp, if you look up toward heaven and heaven seems deaf, then stop looking toward heaven and look toward humanity. You can't have a great spiritual experience again until you have given the One you *do* have to someone else.

That may mean sacrifice. It may mean moving out of your comfortable home. It may mean going where there is great need. Many a man who had been going dry spiritually has gone down to the slums and found Christ waiting for him there, and his soul has soared once more . . .

The water of life will flow to us only if it flows *through* us. You can't keep it unless you give it away. You can't even have it. The greatest thing in the world changes color and taste even while you hold it. Let go of it quickly—pass it on. God is love, and love is what pours through. Love does not mean self-love. The moment a man tries to keep God to himself he ceases to have love; he has only self-love. Love is love only if it passes on (B. pp. 71, 72).

A WORD
TO THE WISE

The letter killeth, but the spirit giveth life (II Corinthians 3:6b).

Many people suspect religious piety today because it may be a camouflage for selfishness. It is not worse than the situation in the business world, but then the business world does not pretend to be pious or unselfish. Business, at least, is honest about that. Too much of Christianity professes to believe in being unselfish when it is in reality selfish; any ordinary person sees through its shallow hypocrisy. That we are rich and "respectable" blinds us to the fact that in the eyes of heaven we are rather contemptible.

We all tend to become like the Pharisee in the temple who spent his prayer hour thanking God that he was not like other people and spent none of that hour praying for other people.

Others could go to hell, as far as he cared. Indeed, it gave him an ugly sense of superiority to think that he was going where they could not go. We loathe his kind. Those sects in the Christian Church and those people in the Christian Church who think that they only will be saved for their orthodoxy, while the rest go to hell, do not know they are carrying into their religion the Pharisee's selfish desire to triumph over others. It is all the more loathesome because they are so unctuous about it.

So we are caught between two kinds of self-centeredness—the one secular, the other religious. Our religion is little because we are little . . . .

It was always true that we could not get into the kingdom of heaven unless we took everyone we could with us. But that truth is hard for people to realize. Today it is easier for people to realize that our world threatens to come crashing around our heads unless we work and pray for other people (B. pp. 106, 107).

CHRIST SATISFIES
OUR INFINITE LONGINGS

My God shall supply all your need according to his riches in glory by Christ Jesus (Philippians 4:19).

Within all of us a tension is set up by the fact that the body is limited, while the soul has limitless longings which cannot be satisfied through the body. We aspire for infinitely more than we can reach. The difference between our reach and our aim is as vast as the difference between the reach of the arm and the reach of vision as it peers into the depths of space. As bodies, we are worms creeping about on the bottom of an ocean of air, more restricted than the fish, for they can soar at will through their atmosphere of water as easily as we walk. The human body quickly strikes its limit. After a few years it shrivels and decays. This creeping, aching, dying machine excites the admiration of physiologists perhaps, but it does not satisfy the human soul. Nothing that earth offers satisfies it permanently . . .

An Indian Christian said, "Christ both satisfies and dissatisfies us, for He fills us with new wants." This is indeed what experience teaches. To have Him gives a deep peace, yet to see Him in His perfect beauty leaves us dissatisfied; dissatisfied not because of things we do not possess, but with our own selves. We cease to blame the universe, but we do not cease to aspire.

But there is this great difference. Now those nameless, mysterious longings which we had before take definite form. We long to be like Him, to help others be like Him, to be closer to Him, and to help others to be closer to Him (F. pp. 163, 165, 166).

MAN'S DILEMMA CHALLENGES US

Put on the whole armour of God, that ye may be able to stand against the wiles of the devil (Ephesians 6:11).

So man's dilemma challenges you and me, and God challenges you and me to help our age push its spiritual knowledge ahead five hundred years.

I for one am accepting that challenge in dead earnest. I for one am determined to go the whole way. I for one promise God that by His help I will believe the revelation of Christ, all of it, believe with all my life and will, as well as with my mind. And there are an ever-increasing number of Christians who are making this tremendous resolution.

If you accept this challenge with us, and resolve to prove the power of faith and prayer and utter obedience, then the first thing to do is to make contact with the other men and women who are making this tremendous resolution and are carrying it out in minute-by-minute living. There are many such people, most of whom fail to share their deepest experiences with others . . .

Jesus said that His miracles were possible because of the faith of those who were cured. Only in His home town, Nazareth, did He fail to cure diseases, "because of their unbelief." "According to your faith be it unto you"—this was what He said. Every doctor will tell you that there are laws of health, and that you will suffer if you break them, whether you know those laws or not. This, many of us are convinced, applies to the spiritual laws of health, whether we know those laws or not. The medical profession has gone a long way in this direction in the past few years. Many physicians now attribute stomach ulcers to a depressed unhappy state of mind—caused by resentment or discouragement or fear—which pours too much irritating acid into the stomach. Much arthritis and heart disease is now attributed by physicians to an unhealthful state of mind pouring unwholesome secretions into the body. On the other hand, faith and hope and joy and love hasten cures. This we now know—and it is new knowledge! We have gone so far in this direction in such a short time that no one dares guess where this connection of mind and body really ends. I call it "new knowledge," but it is really the first step toward agreeing with Jesus. It is old to Him (H. pp. 7, 8).

CONSTANTLY
ABIDING

I have set the LORD always before
me: because he is at my right hand,
I shall not be moved (Psalm 16:8).

A devotional hour is no substitute for "constantly abiding,"
but it is an indispensible help; it starts the day right.

But the day must be kept right. We should cultivate the habit
of turning to God whenever we stop any piece of work and look
around to ask what to do next. Those little interim moments are
priceless.

It is not necessary to pray long prayers; a fraction of a second
is enough. It is a wonderful thing to shoot silent flash prayers at
people whom we meet. If we are sitting in a church or a rail-
road train, it is good to pray for the people who are around
us. It is good to cultivate the habit of taking walks with God. It
is good to talk to Him when dressing, when in the bathroom.
We can be whispering to our Father as we fall asleep in bed.
When we awaken in the morning or lean back to rest on our
chair for a moment we can talk with Him. Every one of these
moments can be a time for recharging our spiritual batteries.

The great prayer masters devoted all, or nearly all, of their
waking hours to prayer. That does not mean that they did
nothing else; it means that they prayed and worked simultan-
eously. They prayed while they read, while they walked, while
they listened to music, while they were writing, while they
were working with their hands. They shared all they did and all

they thought and all they said with God, and thus they could engage in a busy life and yet "pray without ceasing."

As one continues to practice this presence of God, his thoughts seem to grow progressively better, more fruitful than they were when he began. Some people give it up because at first it produces only a few scattered thoughts, and they seem not to be very valuable. It is like changing over on the typewriter from the one finger "hunt-and-peck method" to the touch system; anyone who has tried that knows that it is not easy. The old way keeps breaking in on the new. So it is with stopping this desultory, foggy, contact with God which we have been practicing, as we strive for a "constant abiding" (B. pp. 95, 96, 97).

THE UNIVERSAL CHRIST

He (Christ) is both the first principle and the upholding principle of the whole scheme of creation (Colossians 1:17, Phillips).

The two billions of people on this globe differ greatly in their tastes, hungers and needs. To each person Christ offers a type of friendship best suited to his needs. All these types are right, but none can say, "I alone am right."

Millions of people of all churches have had such an intense experience of Christ that they are classified among the mystics. In point of fact, *everyone* is a mystic, if he believes that God answers back when he prays. Most of us are mystics occasionally, but a true mystic believes that he hears God answering back habitually, and perhaps all the time . . .

Evelyn Underhill calls mysticism the way of "life which aims at communion with God." A mystic "aims," pushes his will toward God, just as all of us do when we experience conversion. He does not differ in essence from the rest of us at our very best; save that he seeks God more continuously than we do, and so finds more of him, for the reason that "he that seeketh findeth."

There is as much variety among mystics as there is among the rest of us. 1. To some of them God's message seems to be intellectual. St. John of the Cross, Eckhart and Dante illustrate this type. 2. To some God comes as intense love. St. Theresa, St. Francis, and Walter Hinton illustrate this type. 3. To some mystics God gives power. St. Augustine, John Wesley, George Fox, and Wordsworth belong here. To be sure the great mystics have had all these experiences—illumination, emotion, and power—but they differed in the emphasis which they placed upon each of these.

The mystical love between Christ and the soul does indeed resemble the love of man and wife at its highest and best. But the highest love-experience with Christ, in its white-hot, crystal-pure intensity, far transcends any other love this world knows (F. pp. 171, 172, 173).

PAYING THE
SUPREME PRICE

Whosoever he be of you that for-
saketh not all that he hath, he cannot
be my disciple (Luke 14:33).

If one has paid the supreme price so that he can say, "Fade,
fade, each earthly joy, Jesus is mine," then one begins to ex-
plore a new and wonderful world. Our ultimate satisfaction does
not depend upon the material things of this world which we
inhabit at the moment. Rather it depends upon the training we
receive to appreciate the things of the spiritual world. As we
learn to love the Master with an ever-deeper devotion, we find
an ever-greater joy in His constant presence. "In the secret of
His presence, how my soul delights to hide." Our joy is in exact
proportion to our love of being with Him. He is incomparably
more lovable than any other person, and so the delight of His
love may become a hundred times more glorious than the pleasure we may derive from any other friendship.

The twofold price we must pay for this "pearl of great price"
is: First, to become spiritually minded, with the mind engrossed
in the things on the spirit level, not engrossed with material
things, and: Second, to love Christ with all the soul and mind
and heart and strength.

For perfect friendship with Jesus is a glorious affair. Why
does that infatuated youth tingle from head to foot while he is
with his sweetheart? Because nature made him to love and
every cell in his body responds. That and far more is the ecstasy

of those who are infatuated with Jesus. Nature made them for Him and every fiber in their bodies responds.

If we abandon "the world, the flesh, and the devil" and fix our affections on Jesus, words fail to express the glory, the rapture of His warm intimacy, the gentle purity of His close love (F. pp. 170, 171).

LIFE MORE ABUNDANTLY

The thief cometh not, but for to steal, and to kill, and to destroy: I am come that they might have life, and that they might have it more abundantly (John 10:10).

One of the chief rewards of the friendship of Jesus is *life*, as the Bible constantly reiterates. "You must think of yourselves as dead to sin but alive to God, through union with Christ Jesus." "And this is life eternal, that they might know thee, the only true God, and Jesus Christ, whom thou hast sent."

When a lawyer wanted to know what to do to "inherit eternal life," Jesus' answer contained a significant omission—he left out the word "eternal." The lawyer had asked:

"Master, what shall I do to inherit *eternal* life?"

Jesus replied: "What is written in the law? How readest thou?"

The lawyer quoted: "Thou shalt love the Lord thy God with all thy heart, and with all thy soul, and with all thy strength, and with all thy mind; and thy neighbor as thyself."

Jesus said: "Thou hast answered right: this do, and thou shalt *live."* He did not say, "Thou shalt have eternal life," for Jesus did not think the lawyer had ever been alive. Jesus meant, "This do and thou shalt *begin to live."* That existence which the lawyer called "life" was not in Jesus' opinion worth continuing forever, neither for himself, nor for God. When Nicodemus came to talk one night, Jesus said: "Ye must be born again . . . Except a man be born again he cannot enter into the kingdom of God." "I am come," said Jesus at another time, "that they might have life, and . . . have it more abundantly" (F. pp. 151, 152).

THE MORE
EXCELLENT WAY

Covet earnestly the best gifts: and yet shew I unto you a more excellent way (I Corinthians 12:31).

One method of building character common in schools is to prepare a list of desirable qualities and ask students to check themselves by that list. The weakness of this process is that it intensifies self-centeredness. If students take the list too seriously and find themselves failing to live up to it, they develop a morbid sense of defeat. Such lists have exactly the same defect as Paul said the Mosaic law had. Either they are easy and therefore inadequate lists, or else they leave one with a keen awareness of moral failure.

The queen of all virtues, the virtue which makes heaven heavenly, is to be a worthy member of a society of selves lost in love like the love of Christ. Paul says, "I will show you a more excellent way," and then gives us the most magnificent treatise on love in all literature. "If I have all other virtues," he declares, "and have not love, I am nothing." Probing inside ourselves for sins and weaknesses does not beget love of others, but only self-love.

The "more excellent way" is to fall in love intimately with Jesus. If we do that it will not be necessary for us to worry about our character. If we keep "looking unto Jesus" the change will take place of itself. Our line of action is simple—forget ourselves, let go, focus our attention upon Jesus, and trust everything to Him. If we continue to admire Him and to imitate Him day by day, the change will take place inside us without introspection. Nathaniel Hawthorne has revealed this in that wonderful classic *The Great Stone Face*. The youth Ernest gazed lovingly day after day at the beautiful stone face against the Vermont mountains until at last he himself caught the purity and serenity and nobility of that lovely visage (F. pp. 144, 145, 146).

PRAY FOR WORLD LEADERS

I exhort therefore, that first of all, supplications, prayers, intercessions, and giving of thanks, be made for all men (I Timothy 2:1).

Prayer is needed as it was never needed in all history, that leaders may become large enough soon enough. The men planning for a united world have been intensely patriotic *national* leaders, and their viewpoints are inevitably warped by their love of country. They love their own people passionately, and as a rule have prejudices against other peoples, and so instinctively grasp for national advantages . . .

A shower of prayers, gentle as snow, must fall upon these

leaders in every nation to save them from being jealous, suspicious, greedy, prejudiced, full of resentment and hatred, and from driving bargains with weaker peoples which will later breed trouble . . .

We must pray for Congress and particularly for senators, for they have in their hands the stupendous power of ratifying or rejecting treaties. We ought to write to the senators of our own state and to our own congressmen, telling them that we are praying for them. The letters of the most obscure people are read in Washington. Elective officers pay more attention to those who vote for them than to anyone else.

We must pray for the leaders of England and the House of Commons, for the leaders in Russia, for the French, for Chinese authorities and for all others who may emerge into positions of power in this rapidly changing world.

If we pray for them ten seconds several times a day we shall be more likely to secure results than if we prayed once for half an hour. An excellent practice is to stop for ten seconds while reading the newspapers and pray for any person who is likely to affect world affairs. Suppose ten million people read their newspapers and prayed for every important person and event! If ten million ought to do this, you and I must—we must lead so that they will follow (E. pp. 21, 22).

WE CAN
WIN THE WORLD

I am made all things to all men,
that I might by all means save some
(I Corinthians 9:22b).

We could conquer the world's heart by serving it, as Jesus said we should. But in this all-out attack of help, the Church has a very basic responsibility. It must find the right kind of men.

The technicians will fail unless they have the type of character that the Church at its best produces: men with high honor, good habits, integrity, warm heart, Christlike compassionate desire to help—democratic and congenial men who are "color blind," loving, and beloved.

Such men would do as much to raise the ideals of people as they would to teach skills. They would be living witnesses for Christ, and living witnesses for America at her best . . .

This is 100 per cent the way of Christ, and who said that anyone in trouble is our neighbor; so help him and love him.

This is the only way to convert Russia to the way of Christ.

As surprising world-wide kindness wins the nations, the Communists in Russia will see that violence and hate die out like a candle against loving service, and they will change over to our weapons. Then we shall have a war of kindness to conquer the heart of the world! Who could ask more? (I. pp. 9, 11).

To worship nightly is to love each other,
Each smile a hymn, each kindly deed a prayer.
—Whittier

LAYING UP
TREASURES IN HEAVEN

> Lay up for yourselves treasures in heaven, where neither moth nor rust doth corrupt, and where thieves do not break through nor steal (Matthew 6:20).

The way to lay up a treasure in heaven is to help human need. It is the only way that Jesus ever gave us. What we hold we lose, what we use to help others is ours forever . . .

If true, this is enormously urgent. It is too urgent to be thrown aside without careful study. Too urgent not to press upon the attention of everyone you know. It may decide the issue of survival.

You will not like all of this book; some of it will sting and hurt you. But when you have finished, you will see a glorious vision, you will know the only answer to our dilemma, and you will see that answer within your grasp, for you will be part of the answer.

Here is the way, the only way to save our country, our world, and our loved ones from being swept over the brink of unthinkable horror.

So let it hurt! Your pain is part of the birth pangs of a new world . . .

But I do worry. My heart and soul and mind burn to save America and the world from being struck by an atom bomb. Especially am I excited because the true way to peace and survival is precisely the Way of Christ. This book is a lesson in applied Christianity, all of it, though it may sound too practical

90

and self-evident for religion. But Jesus was practical and self-evident, if only people had been wise enough to try Him (I. pp. 12, 15).

FACING TODAY'S
CHALLENGE

> This know also that in the last days perilous times shall come.
>
> For men shall be lovers of their own selves, covetous, boasters, proud, blasphemers, disobedient to parents, unthankful, unholy . . .
>
> Having a form of godliness, but denying the power thereof: from such turn away (II Timothy 3:1, 2, 5).

The past century has been weak in deep religious faith. This is due partly to the critical attitude toward the Bible, partly to the skepticism among teachers in colleges, partly to the exclusion of religion from the public schools, and probably most of all due to the intense, fast-moving life people live, which gives them no time for prayer or meditation. The high-pressure "care of this world, and the deceitfulness of riches, choke the word"—as does the deceitfulness of *seeking* riches!

Our peril today lies in just this, that we are in a new low spiritual depression—in power, in faith, in prayer, and in love. A similar condition prevailed in Germany—and Hitler became possible. Our depression of faith today is worldwide.

For example, a well-known minister thought that I should omit the gospel of John from my *Story of Jesus* because "we have rejected that gospel"! If that minister had a full spiritual experience, I think that he would call John the most profound book in the Bible and in the world. Only in the gospel of John can one begin faintly to *understand* Jesus. There and there alone does one discover the secret of Jesus' power . . . Obedience that led Him to Jerusalem to die. When they lied about Him, spat on Him, drove the frightful nails through His wrists and ankles, dropped His cross into the hole causing intolerable agony, drew lots for His clothes while He hung quivering with pain, His obedience never wavered, not even when He gave that last terrible loud cry, "My God, my God, why hast thou forsaken me?" During the moment when His Father seemed to abandon Him, Jesus remained true to God. It was obedience *at whatever cost* (H. pp. 3, 4, 5).

NEW SPIRITUAL
DISCOVERIES

I count not myself to have apprehended: but this one thing I do, forgetting those things which are behind, and reaching forth unto those things which are before,

I press toward the mark for the prize of the high calling of God in Christ Jesus (Philippians 3:13, 14).

The scientists themselves urge man to catch up spiritually with their scientific discoveries; for the awful power they have put in man's hands, at his present spiritual level, is as certain as the sunrise to bring unspeakable disaster to the whole human race. To me this spells a tremendous challenge, and I believe it should mean the same to every Christian. We must make spiritual progress in great strides, or it will not come in time. I for one pledge myself, before my fellow men and God, to do all I can from this time forth to help make this spiritual advance possible. If you who read these words join with me in this pledge, we must use the methods of the scientists: we must plunge into spiritual experiments with all our powers, and exchange our findings with one another. Just as science was driven by desperate necessity to push physics ahead "five hundred years," so we are driven by desperate necessity to try to push our spiritual level ahead five hundred years (H. pp. 3, 4).

We need fresh, daring spiritual discoveries, whole continents of them, and we need them terribly. We need a new wideness, a world-wideness. When men will to see God only through the narrow slit science may offer, they see nothing but an "oblong blur" (A. p. 82).

In the realm of the spirit, immense devotion is needed: untiring concentration of the heart upon God, building upon all the achievements of the spiritual giants of the past, and pooling and evaluating the results of our inch-by-inch advances in our conquest of what to us is the spiritually unknown.

Some theologian may object that we can make no new spiritual discoveries, that Jesus Christ knew all. I agree, but who will pretend to understand what Jesus Christ really meant? The life of every one of us every day is a flat contradiction of what He said. What, for example, did Jesus say about healing disease by the power of faith? What did He do? He healed them all! Instantly! Not one Christian out of a million ever heals anyone by prayer. Who will contradict by statement that we are all weak, where He urged us to be triumphant? We don't have His secret (H. p. 4).

URGENTLY NEEDED
EXPERIMENTS WITH PRAYER

Seek, and ye shall find; knock, and
it shall be opened unto you (Matthew
7:7b).

There is one vital difference between the experiments of the
physicists with atoms and our experiments with prayer. The
physicist in his work looks on from the outside of matter while
he experiments, but the man of prayer works within the depths
of his own soul. Others may look on from the outside and see
diseases melt away, or the development of plants occurring
much more rapidly than ordinarily (an achievement reported
by Professor Rhine), but the spiritual experiment itself must be
tried in the secret chambers of one's own soul. This makes it
more difficult for the observer to study prayer from the outside.
He can see the results, but he may not be able to determine
why the prayer of one man works miracles and the prayer of
another man lacks the mysterious power to do the impossible.
Prayer cannot be weighed or measured or tested with a Geiger
counter. This situation presents a disadvantage.

On the other hand it presents a great advantage, because
anyone who is willing to make the effort can test it for himself.
He requires no laboratory with expensive equipment, for his
laboratory is his own soul, and he finds human needs of every
kind waiting for his prayer to make things right. You, if you are
a sincere Christian, can become a spiritual scientist where you
are. I do not mean by adopting some different theory, like
Christian Science or Vedanta; I mean by simply testing whether

the kind of prayer Jesus practiced and taught does today what He was able to do. You can prove whether He told the truth, by fulfilling His conditions. And that is the most vital question in the world today.

If Jesus were wrong, then we face annihilation. If He were right, then we must become right, or perish. We who pray are more important than the greatest scientist who does not pray. He can destroy mankind. We can save it, if Jesus told the truth. If Jesus told the truth, then the Christians of our day live a lie in which all of us are caught; for we deny His truth in our lives while we preach it with our tongues. Almost no preacher has enough faith to practice what He reads to his congregation from the gospels on Sunday morning. Few preachers have the faith even to *preach* what they read from the gospels. And yet the Gospel must be proven true in our day, or we shall perish (H. p. 6).

IT PAYS TO BE
A GOOD NEIGHBOR

Thou shalt love the Lord thy God with all thy heart, and with all thy soul, and with all thy strength, and with all thy mind; and thy neighbour as thyself (Luke 10:27).

America has had enough experience, if we profit by it, to know that one dollar invested in being a good neighbor brings as much return as a thousand dollars invested in guns and bombs. Indeed, the good-neighbor program has been a marvelous success wherever it has been carried out by sincere, kindhearted men. It fails only when we try to substitute loans of money and to work from a distance instead of sending warm-hearted friends (I. p. 95).

Japan is one of the most striking illustrations in the world of how a nation can change from hate to love in two years. At the end of World War II they hated us bitterly. Then MacArthur, who understood Japan, instead of punishing the Japanese, did his best to give them good government and to help them to recover. His kindness was so surprising that public opinion turned a somersault. When the vote was taken in 1949 to determine what nation was most popular among Japanese, the United States got ten times as many votes as any other nation and more than all the others put together. It paid to be a good neighbor to Japan.

But had we stayed away and merely loaned Japan a billion dollars, as we have often done for other countries, she would not have loved us. A good neighbor doesn't lend us money; a good neighbor goes and lends a hand (I. p. 100).

Unless we help people to help themselves, the Voice of America and the Crusade for Freedom are utterly futile as substitutes for this help . . . Deeds—compassionate helpfulness plus witness, these two—will save the world if they are done by men who love their fellow men. And this is pure Christlikeness. That is why the Church should take the leading part, because only Christians can do this with perfectly Christian love (I. pp. 110, 111).

OUR CHANGING
WORLD

Heaven and earth shall pass away:
but my words shall not pass away
(Luke 21:33).

Jesus asked the impossible in the year 30, but it is possible in
the 1960's.

His last words after His Resurrection were: "Go and make
disciples of all nations ... You shall be my witnesses to the end
of the earth . . ." Under the stupendous intoxication of the Holy
Spirit at Pentecost, they went out and tried—how they tried!
Philip, Paul, Silas, Peter, Mark, Barnabas, Timothy, Prisca,
Aquila, Silvanus, John and Apollos, and thousands upon thousands of others tried and died trying. They took sailing boats
westward on the Mediterranean; they followed the Roman
roads westward into all Europe. In two centuries they captured
the Roman Empire! . . .

. . . His disciples could go to all the Roman Empire, but *they*
could not go to "all the world."

Now *we* can! The airplane and helicopter, the steamship, or
the bus reach everywhere. Now we can "go to all the world and
preach the gospel to every creature—if the governments will let
us in. And nearly all of them will. In fact, they need us!

A combination of circumstances make this the *first* period
since Jesus gave His great command when we could really carry
it out (J. pp. 9, 10).

Bringing the world to Christ and His way is more important

than all the other education the world may receive. To this, I suppose, every dedicated Christian will agree.

So it is essential *for the Church* to train and send men and women who can reveal the love of Christ in their hearts by relieving suffering and meeting need, as Jesus did, and then witnessing for Jesus and His kingdom purpose. They need a "Prince of Peace Corps" (J. p. 40).

COMMUNISM
CHALLENGES CHRISTIANS

Watch ye, stand fast in the faith, quit you like men, be strong (I Corinthians 16:13).

It is clear that God is using the Communist threat to *awaken our churches* to do far more for the world. We Christians have been complacent and asleep, supposing that our magnificent cathedrals could take the place of compassion in fulfilling Christ's command.

God is using this crisis to put us and the thirty million native Christians to work. They too have been complacent, "asleep in Zion," letting a few do all the witnessing, while the vast majority were drones "being done good," getting their own souls saved.

God is using this crisis to tell the missionaries that in missions there has been too much *preaching* without enough *practicing*. Missionaries must adopt our "Each One Teach One and Win One"—first *practice* the compassion of Jesus, then tell how much Jesus loves every lost man. The story of the compassionate love of Jesus has sounded incredibly beautiful, too good to be true, to the starving non-Christian. But when his teacher loves him just as Jesus would, he believes! It is true! It is true! Oh, God, it is true! For he has seen Jesus in the love of his teacher. Unless practice matches words, people do not believe our words (J. pp. 17, 18).

While "each one teach one" began thirty-five years ago as a way to teach and win non-Christians in illiterate areas, it now begins to reveal immensely wider possibilities as a means of witnessing for Jesus (J. p. 21).

The airplane, the population explosion, the Communist threat, our easy-to-teach lessons, are all God at work. When I see how God is using even the Communists when they deny His existence, I feel like exclaiming, "Oh, the depth of the riches and wisdom and knowledge of God. How unsearchable are his judgments" (J. p. 17).

OUR GREATEST
OPEN DOOR

Behold, I have set before thee an open door, and no man can shut it (Revelation 3:8).

We who believe that He is Lord and Master have no doubt that He will triumph. But this does not mean that we and America are sure to be in His kingdom, just because we said, "Lord, Lord." He wept over Jerusalem because He foresaw the doom which fell upon her forty years later. Unless America learns how to reach out in compassion and lift the world out of its misery, helping it help itself up, we are going to suffer the fate of Jerusalem in forty years, for the hate wave against us is rising higher each year.

Many Americans say, "See how much we have already done for the world!"

Our government tried to do much, but found that because of the sovereignty of nations she could not, as a government, enter other countries and do it for them . . .

The Church is able to do the very things the government cannot do. The foreign governments need our help in lifting and satisfying the masses so much that they will permit us to enter their countries and teach their people, and witness that we are doing it because we learned it from Christ. When we do that we are bearing witness, not only to the illiterates whom we teach, but also to aristocracy who will be watching us do what they have never done. The only way to save the world for Christ, and for what we call our "free way of life," is to set the world an example (J. pp. 66, 67).

Service without witness is inadequate, witness without service lacks the power to convince. What we do for people verifies what we say. What we say tells them *why we do it*.

Prayer, plus loving service, plus witness, is the irresistible trinity that wins as marvelously as Jesus won in His day (J. p. 40).

NEEDED: A
MASTER OPPORTUNITY

I sought for a man among them,
that should make up the hedge, and
stand in the gap before me for the
land, that I should not destroy it: but
I found none (Ezekial 22:30).

When John R. Mott was leading the Church at the turn of the century he was called a "master of opportunity." We need him now, for today the Church is "bungling opportunity," blind before the greatest open door in history.

Half the people in our churches are frustrated, bewildered, willing to help the world, but at a loss to know how. Another half, discouraged at the failure of government aid, wants to draw into their shell and forget the world; those who favor isolation will not go along with those who favor a larger share for the Church.

Since the people are so divided, the "unified budget" cannot be changed enough soon enough!

The only hope is "specials," over and beyond the unified budget, by that half of the Church who believe in reaching around the world. The most successful way we have tried thus far is to organize "Companies of Compassion" of those who will contribute $1.00 a week. If one hundred persons in a church or community give a dollar a week, that will total $5200 in a year, enough to provide for a man and his wife abroad, or for the publication of *The Story of Jesus,* or other graded books (J. pp. 68, 69).

In what way can your church get the "Each One Teach One

and Win One to Christ" objective carried out? Our Laubach Literacy Fund is trained to help you, and we are ready.

All we need are hundreds of "Companies of Compassion" to set our wings free ...

We are asking world-visioned Americans who have been blessed with abundance to provide enough so that we can say "yes" instead of "no" to the appeals of these one hundred nations. With your partnership we can become potent enough, with God's blessing (and this is what God wants) to intervene and change the present shocking crumbling of American influence in the world (J. pp. 70, 71).

OUR SECURITY FOR TIME AND ETERNITY

For after that in the wisdom of God the world by wisdom knew not God, it pleased God by the foolishness of preaching to save them that believe (I Corinthians 1:21).

If teaching men how to read and leading them to modern technology were enough, my soul would sing the doxology. But this has me terrified. For they need Christ in their hearts to make knowledge safe in their heads and power safe in their hands.

We who associate with men and women who have been changed by the loveliness of Jesus, often assume that theirs and ours is the viewpoint of all the rest of mankind. But it is dangerous illusion ... The world leaders who are not controlled by the way of Christ are thinking thoughts and plotting plots which are horribly unsafe when they have the power of Jove's thunderbolt in atomic energy at the beck and call of their selfish plans. The world is unsafe without Christ. The more it knows, the more unsafe it becomes.

So we need to keep reminding ourselves that in our witness for Jesus Christ we have not only the best hope for eternity for each soul, but the only hope for the future of this world. This is why *the Church must teach*. Education is fine *if* it is Christ directed. *It is evil if it is directed by evil.* It only adds to the peril and evil of the world if it is under the control of demonic minds. Education is good only if people are good . . .

Is science good? Yes, if those who use it are motivated by the ideals of Jesus Christ. It is evil if those who use it are motivated by small, selfish, revengeful purposes. Science in itself is neither good or evil, it is a servant of humanity. Whether its result is good or evil depends upon whether "humanity" is good or evil (J. pp. 41, 42).

The Church has the stupendous and even terrifying responsibility to produce men with conscience, passion to serve, sterling integrity, and true technical skill, and it must see that such men are used all over the world. The church must lift not only the minds of men, but also their souls, their integrity, their love (I. p. 150).